D1537622

VIENNA

IMPERIAL CITY

CENTRO STAMPA EDITORIALE

plurigraf

PERSEUS

Distributed by

bauer

VERLAG C. BAUER GMBH
Beatrixgasse 3, A 1030 Wien
www.verlagbauer.at

Index

Photographs: Archiv Verlag Bauer - Archivio Plurigraf - Laura Ronchi - Tony Stone - Grazia Neri - Gerolimetto – Austrian National Tourist Board (Rome) - Favretto - Bianchi - Sperandei - Marka - Stradella. *Text:* Othmar F. Freudenthaler.
Map published by permission of Freytag - Berndt u. Artaria, Wien
CASA EDITRICE PERSEUS Collezione PLURIGRAF
Published and printed by Centro Stampa Editoriale, Sesto Fiorentino (Firenze).

VIENNA - BRIEF HISTORY OF THE CITY

The oldest evidence of human settlement in the Viennese basin dates back to the Stone Age.

From 400 B.C. onwards the Celts settled here and represented the upper class of a people regarding whom, however, little information is available. In the area of present-day Leopoldsberg, the Celts built one of their typical hill villages and introduced vine-growing. The name "Vedunis" (Waldbach) must have been the Celtic root of the city's subsequent names (Vindobona, Wedunia, Wienne, Vienna).

After the annexation by the Romans in 15 B.C. and the founding of the province of Pannonia, Carnuntum (near Petronell, in northern Austria), it became the capital and a military garrison, but Vindobona (Vienna) became first a military training camp (towards the mid-1st century A.D.) and then, later on, a legionary camp under the Emperor Trajan (98-117).

Emperor Marcus Aurelius, known as the "philosopher", often stayed, as a result of the threat posed by the Marcomanni, at Vindobona and at Carnuntum in the period from 172 to 175, and it was here that he wrote part of his "Reflections".

Towards 213 Vienna became a "municipium", and lived its first golden age under the Severini dynasty. Emperor Probus (276-82) encouraged the development of agriculture and vine-growing and is still today considered to be the founder of the Viennese wine culture.

After the decline of the Western Roman Empire (476), there was a providential intervention by Saint Severino, who died in 482 in Pannonia. In the year 488, Odoacer led the remaining Roman population of the province back to Italy and took the relics of Saint Severino to Naples, which had previously been preserved in the church of Saint James, in the present-day district of Heiligenstadt.

Subsequently, the Longobards and the Slavs settled temporarily in the Viennese basin. In the centuries which followed, raids by the Avars, of Mongol-Tartar origin, and later by the Hungarians, threatened the eastern area of the German kingdom. The "Salzburg Annals" record a battle between the Franks and the Hungarians which must have taken place in 881 "apud Weniam", near Vienna, called for the first time by this name. In 976 the Babenberger line received the Eastern March of the German Empire (Ostmark), which in 996 was officially named 'Ostarrichi'.

Under Saint Leopold III, who reigned from 1095 to 1136 and was canonized in 1485, the foundations were laid for an independent state, and with the elevation of Austria to the status of Duchy (1156), this development was further assured. The first Duke, Henry II Jasomirgott (1141-77), moved his residence to Vienna, while the previous homes of the Babenbergers had been in Melk, Tulln, Gars and Klosterneuburg. In was in this same period, (1147), that the Stephanskirche (Church of Saint Stephen) was consecrated.

Leopold V (1177-94) built Vienna with great munificence, financing the entire project with the ransom mon-

The dates given after rulers' names refer to the period of their reign, rather than to the date of their birth or death.

ey obtained for King Richard the Lionheart of England. By command of Emperor Henry VI, he had been taken prisoner whilst returning to his homeland from a crusade and had then been escorted to Dürnstein.

Vienna, which in 1198 was by right considered to be a city, as well as becoming an important cultural centre of the courtly love song (Minnesang), experienced a significant economic boom, caused partly by the introduction in 1221 of the *Stapelrecht*, the unloading duty, which obliged all travelling merchants either to sell their goods in the city for two months, or otherwise to remove them, but only after payment of a heavy tax.

In 1246 the last descendant of the Babenbergers, Frederick II the Quarrelsome (der Streitbare) died in the battle of Leitha, against the Hungarians. King Otakar II Premysl of Bohemia married Margaret, sister of the

last Babenberger and widow of King Henry VII, thus taking possession of the Duchy. He ordered the construction in Vienna of hospitals, churches and the first nucleus of the Imperial Palace. He died in 1278 at Durnkrut, in the Marchfeld, during the war against the German kingdom over which he had claimed his right. The victor, King Rudolf of Habichtsburg, in the canton of Aargau in Switzerland, introduced the Habsburg dominion to Austria, which was to last for a staggering 640 years and two months.

When Duke Albrecht I, son of Rudolf, refused once more to grant the Viennese their privileges, a rebellion broke out under the first Viennese burgomaster, Konrad Poll (1287-88). The Duke, however, managed to hold sway: from that time onwards, Vienna remained under the control of the reigning prince and obtained

in 1296 a new civic independence, with a document drawn up in German. In the year 1298, Albrecht I was elected as German king, in the presence of the kings of Hungary and Bohemia.

The first of the Habsburgs to consider himself as Viennese was Rudolf IV, the "founder" (1358-65). He vied with his father-in-law, Emperor Charles IV, in the development of the city of Prague and in the improvement of his own residence, Vienna. He earned the nickname of "founder" from the construction of the south tower and the central nave of the Stephanskirche, the foundation of the Alma Mater Rudolfina in 1365, the oldest German University after Prague, with a faculty of Theology from 1385 onwards, and the introduction of the "Privilegium maius", a forged document which set out the privileges of Austria against the law of the kingdom in force at that time (subsequently, the document was actually ratified by Emperor Frederick III in 1453).

In 1396 the citizens of Vienna obtained the "right to elect a council", which gave merchants and artisans the chance to elect each year the burgomaster and the external council. In the first half of the fifteenth century the South Tower of the Stephanskirche, known as S*teffl* (little Stephen), was completed, though not without some difficulty.

From the year 1438 to the year 1806, which signalled the end of the "German Holy Roman Empire", it was always Austrian kings and emperors who ascended to the throne, with an interruption of only three years, from 1742-45.

After the death of the reigning Austrian Prince Ladislas "Posthumus", the posthumous son of Albert V, Emperor Frederick III (1452-93) came into conflict with his brother Albert VI, over issues relating to the succession. At the time the Viennese supported Albert, from whom they expected order and safety, and even besieged the imperial family with their son Maximilian, who was staying in the castle in Vienna, driving them out of the city in an outrageous fashion (1462).

Maximilian, the future emperor, never forgot this offence and, as a "punishment" hardly ever came to Vienna. "His" cities were Innsbruck, Linz and Enns. In the year 1469, Vienna became an independent diocese from Passau, and the Stephanskirche became a cathedral.

King Matthias Hunyadi of Hungary, known as "Corvinus", because of his heraldic symbol depicting a raven, conquered Vienna in 1485 and reigned there as a Renaissance prince, surrounded by artists and humanists, until his death (1490).

Emperor Maximilian I was king from 1486 and emperor from 1508 to 1519. The only son of Frederick III, he reconquered Vienna for the Habsburgs. In 1498 he founded the choir of the "Kapellenknaben", precursor of the Viennese choir "Wiener Sängerknaben" (the Vienna Boys Choir).

Thanks to a brilliant political marriage, he made sure that "the sun would never set" in the kingdom of his grandson Charles V (1519-56, †1558). As a result of his marriage, he himself obtained Burgundy (eastern France, Belgium and the Netherlands). In 1515 during the so-called "First Congress of Vienna", a double wedding took place which resulted from the claims to the throne of Hungary and of Bohemia by the Habsburgs. Maximilian's son, Philip the Fair, obtained Spain and her overseas territories (1516), by marrying Joan of Aragon.

Under Emperor Ferdinand I (†1564), brother of Charles V, the Viennese had to brave the first Turkish occupation (1529). The courage of the defenders, led by Count Niklas Graf Salm and by the burgomaster Treu, combined with the weather conditions (the winter had begun in October), forced Sultan Suleiman to retreat to Hungary.

In those times 80% of the population was Protestant, so that the Reformation represented another serious problem for the emperor. Petrus Canisius was summoned, who made his Jesuits (1551) responsible for the saving of souls and, at the same time, the State forbade Protestants to teach religion in schools (1579); the "Reformation Commissions" of

the succeeding cardinal, Klesl, then implemented a policy to re-Catholicise the Austrian territory. During the Thirty Years' War, (1618-1648), those who decided to remain Protestant, had to leave the city of Vienna, leaving 10% of their goods behind at the time of their departure. In the Vienna of Emperor Leopold I (1658-1705), among other things an excellent composer, the state coffers were in an impoverished state as a result of all the magnificent processions, parades, concerts and operatic performances, the expression of baroque extravagance.

In 1679 half of the Viennese population died (around 100,000 inhabitants) from the plague. "Beloved Augustine", was idolized as a ballad singer and as a symbol of the Viennese will to survive, after he escaped the epidemic, despite the fact that he had been found drunk and asleep on a funeral cart.

From the 13th July to 12th September 1683, Vienna was occupied by the army of Sultan Mehmed IV, under the command of the Grand Vizier Kara Mustafa. The defence of the city was organized by Commander Ernst Rüdiger, Count of Starhemberg, and by the burgomaster Andreas von Liebenberg, and the army of the kingdom succeeded in defeating the invaders at present-day Türkenschanzpark. The failure of this second occupation by the Turks, after that of 1529, averted the possible Islamization of Europe. Subsequently, large areas of the Balkans were also liberated from the Turks: Prince Eugène of Savoy (1663, †1736) distinguished himself in this venture and became the supreme commander of

the army and patron of the arts. Indeed, he used his personal wealth to surround himself with libraries, castles (such as the Belvedere) and collections of works of art. It was in this period that Vienna, after the devastation wrought by the Turks, was consumed by "feverish building activity" and acquired a new baroque aspect. The "kipferl" (a kind of crescent), with its Turkish half-moon shape, is a present-day reminder of the threat of the Turkish siege. Furthermore the Turks, at the time of their retreat, left

their coffee beans behind, and in 1685 the first "Coffee-house" was opened in the city, by now a firmly-established Viennese institution.

In 1713 the plague spread to Vienna once again. The Karlskirche (Church of Saint Carlo Borromeo), one of the sacred buildings most closely connected with the crown, recalls the event.

"Empress" Maria Theresa, who never

had herself crowned and was not, therefore, a "real" empress (1740-80) and her consort, Emperor Francis Stephen of Lorraine (1745-65), still today represent Austria's golden age: they brought about reforms in the field of health and in the civil service, and introduced financial reforms, as well as compulsory education, the abolition of torture during interrogations and conducted a census aimed at determining taxes, contributing in a major way to the country's prosperity. During their reign,

the population of Vienna increased from 130,000 to 200,000 inhabitants. Emperor Joseph II (1765-90), a convinced follower of the Enlightenment, son of Maria Theresa and regent by her side, abolished serfdom and the death penalty, closed those monasteries of an exclusively contemplative, rather than social, nature (secularization), granted equal rights to citizens of various creeds, found-

ed the Court Theatre and the National Theatre, which was subsequently to give rise to the Burgtheater (Imperial Theatre) and forbade, for reasons of hygiene, ostentatious funerals (corpses were taken out of the city immediately and buried in linen sacks and lime); in addition, tombstones were only allowed on the cemetery wall, which is why it is difficult to locate with any certainty the grave belonging to Mozart in the St. Marxer cemetery. Pope Pius VI visited Vienna in 1782, but Joseph II did not, as a result, modify his reforms relating to the church.

After Napoleon Bonaparte was crowned emperor, the German Emperor Francis II, in 1804, also had himself crowned "Austrian Emperor", taking the name Francis I. In 1806, however, he had to relinquish the German crown, since the German kingdom no longer existed as such.

During the Napoleonic Wars, Vienna was occupied in 1805 and in 1809. Both times, Napoleon lodged at Schönbrunn. After having lost many territories as a result of the peace of Schönbrunn, Austria decided to change tactics: through the mediation of Count Metternich in 1810, a marriage was arranged between Francis I's daughter, Marie Louise, and Napoleon himself, who wished to have descendants of noble blood. The issue of this marriage was Napoleon François Joseph Chàrles, Duke of Reichstadt, known in Vienna as "little François", and in France as "l'Aiglon" (the eaglet). He died of tuberculosis at twenty-one years of age at Schönbrunn, when the glory of his father

had waned once and for all and his mother had returned with him to her home-town of Vienna.

Among the musicians of the age let us remember Joseph Haydn (1732-1809), formerly the orchestra conductor in the Esterházy castle in Eisenstadt, composer of the "Gott erhalte..." (anthem to Emperor Francis, whose melody is the basis for the present-day German national anthem). He was the founder of what was superficially defined as "classical music". He died in Vienna in 1809, shortly before the Napoleonic troops occupied the city.

Wolfgang Amadeus Mozart (1756-1791) chose Vienna as his home-town, as did the German Ludwig van Beethoven, native of Bonn (1770-1827), Franz Schubert (1797-1828), Johannes Brahms (1833-1897) and Anton Bruckner (1824-1896). Schönberg, Berg and Webern complete the series of great musical geniuses which was to last until the 20th century and for which Vienna has rightly earned a reputation as the "Capital of Music".

At the time of the second Congress of Vienna the waltz became the "worthy court dance", and the solemn festivities of the congress led the Prince of Lignè to utter the famous words, "this congress is not a meeting, but a dance". It was in these circumstances that Metternich implemented an elaborate system of censorship in Vienna, which provided the fundamental basis for that spirit which later came to be known as the Biedermeier epoch.

The word, both written and spoken, fell under suspicion, and for this reason, poets such as Grillparzer, Raimund and Lenau were noticeably affected. The exception to the rule was Johann Nestroy, who virtuously played with the censorship. Music, including the light variety composed by those such as Lanner and Johann Strauss the Elder, reached remarkable heights at times.

At the "second" Congress of Vienna (1814-15), the European princes rearranged those national boundaries which had been changed during the Napoleonic wars. However, shocking social conditions, the lack of freedom and civil rights, the oppression of entire nations in the multi-ethnic Habsburg state, in addition to the censorship, led, in March 1848, to revolution.

A constitution and the freedom of the press were requested; in Prague the army had to re-establish order, and in Hungary an anti-regime was set up. The Hungarian revolutionary army supported the Viennese revolutionaries, who had taken up arms and barricaded themselves in the court arsenal.

At first the revolutionaries were forced to capitulate before the imperial troops of Prince Windischgrätz and of Jellacic. On a second occasion, however, when they saw the fire of the Hungarian cannons outside the city, they broke the armistice. It was for this reason that the reprisals taken after the defeat of the revolutionaries were particularly bloody.

As a consequence of the revolution of '48, Emperor Ferdinand I was forced to abdicate in favour of Francis Joseph I. Vienna remained occupied until 1853.

With the incorporation of the suburbs of Vienna as far as the "Liniewall" (corresponding to the present-day Gürtel sector) into the municipality of the city, the population of Vienna reached 431,000 inhabitants.

With the construction of a new arsenal on the lines of a fortress, it was hoped to prevent the people from taking up arms so easily in future, as had been the case in 1848.

In 1854 Francis Joseph married Elizabeth of Bavaria, known affectionately by the people as "Sissy". After the death of her son, Crown Prince Rudolf (who committed suicide at Mayerling on 30th January 1889), she led a restless life, travelling widely, and in 1898 was the victim of an assassination attempt by the anarchist Luigi Luccheni, in Geneva. The emperor, on the other hand, found an intelligent twin soul in the court actress Katharina Schratt.

In addition to a phase of Neo-absolutism which was designed to keep the peace in the Austrian-Hungarian territories, Francis Joseph introduced a series of "fin-de-siècle projects"

which substantially changed the face of the city: with the elimination of the bastions, which were obstructing modern urbanistic development, it was made possible to build the Ringstrasse (ring-road), the Opera House, the Court Theatre, the university etc. in an architectural style which became known as the Ringstrasse style.

The plan for regulating the Danube lessened the danger of flooding; with the construction of two aqueducts which led from the upper basins of the Rax and the Schneeberg, the danger of cholera was eliminated once and for all; at the Wiener Weltausstellung (Viennese World Exhibition) in the year 1873, Vienna was revealed as a great economic and cultural power. The music sector, too, played a very important role: almost half the world's population in this "golden age of operetta" gave itself up to the romantic waltzes of Johann Strauss the Younger (1825-99), Franz von Suppé, Millocker and Zeller.

Towards 1890 Vienna numbered 1.4 million inhabitants, 10.3% of whom consisted of Jews, to whom the city owed a large part of its cultural splendour.

With the foundation of the "Secession" in 1897, whose building, constructed for the Exhibition, was designed by J. Olbrich as a "Temple to the Jugendstil", many famous artists, including Gustav Klimt in particular, freed themselves from the academic spirit of their time. In

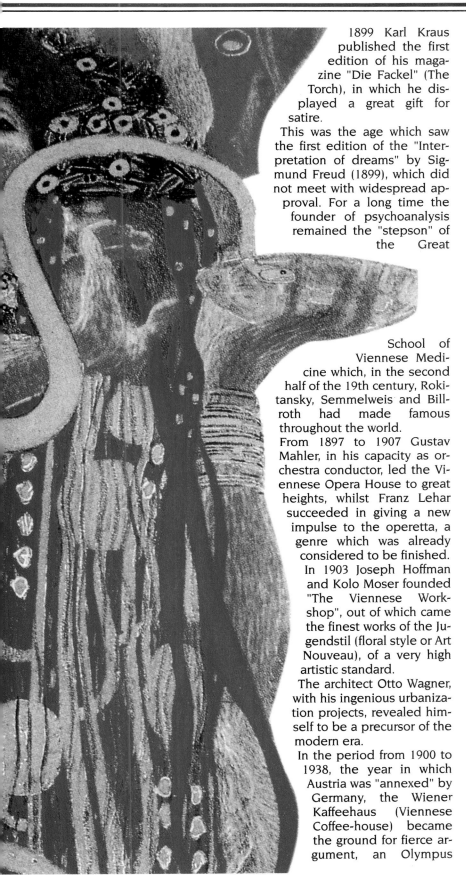

1899 Karl Kraus published the first edition of his magazine "Die Fackel" (The Torch), in which he displayed a great gift for satire.

This was the age which saw the first edition of the "Interpretation of dreams" by Sigmund Freud (1899), which did not meet with widespread approval. For a long time the founder of psychoanalysis remained the "stepson" of the Great School of Viennese Medicine which, in the second half of the 19th century, Rokitansky, Semmelweis and Billroth had made famous throughout the world.

From 1897 to 1907 Gustav Mahler, in his capacity as orchestra conductor, led the Viennese Opera House to great heights, whilst Franz Lehar succeeded in giving a new impulse to the operetta, a genre which was already considered to be finished.

In 1903 Joseph Hoffman and Kolo Moser founded "The Viennese Workshop", out of which came the finest works of the Jugendstil (floral style or Art Nouveau), of a very high artistic standard.

The architect Otto Wagner, with his ingenious urbanization projects, revealed himself to be a precursor of the modern era.

In the period from 1900 to 1938, the year in which Austria was "annexed" by Germany, the Wiener Kaffeehaus (Viennese Coffee-house) became the ground for fierce argument, an Olympus dominated by clouds of smoke and *Weltanschauung* for the great spirits of the age in the fields of culture and politics. It is here that world literature was born. Names such as Schnitzler, Rilke, Trakl, Molnar, Polgar, Kuh, Fridell, Altenberg, Torberg and Werfel will always remain linked with this essentially Viennese atmosphere, now gone forever.

The death of Emperor Francis Joseph at Schönbrunn in 1916, during the First World War, heralded the terminal decline of the splendour of ancient Austria. Two years later his successor Charles I, having lost the war, was forced to renounce his title. Austria became a republic. The social-democrat Karl Seits, in his capacity as the mayor of "red" Vienna (1923-34), ordered the construction of 60,000 new flats (the "Karl Marx Hof" for example), which were funded by building taxes.

During the Second World War around 13% of the city of Vienna was destroyed. The "jeep 4" (4 soldiers of the 4 victorious powers for each patrol vehicle) became the symbol of the fourfold occupation. In 1955 the Minister for Foreign Affairs, Figl, from the balcony of the Belvedere, showed a large and enthusiastic crowd of people, the "*Staatsvertrag*" (State Treaty) which gave Austria back its freedom.

In the cold war Vienna played an important part in the negotiations between east and west, as is shown by the summit between Kennedy and Kruschev in 1961 and the signing of the Salt treaty between Carter and Brezhnev.

Since 1979, as the third seat of the United Nations, after Geneva and New York, and as the seat of several International Organizations (International Authority for Atomic Energy, IAEA since 1957, OPEC since 1965, United Nations Organization for Industrial Development, UNIDO since 1967...) and thanks in addition to its geographical position, after the fall of the "Eisernen Vorhang" (Iron Curtain), the city of Vienna, with its 1.6 million inhabitants, has won back its ancient role as an eastern city in the west, or the "bulwark of the west".

STEPHANSDOM

(CATHEDRAL OF SAINT STEPHEN)
(Stephansdom Square 1)

Under the Babenberger Duke, Henry II Jasomirgott, immediately outside the Romanesque walls which characterize and dominate the city, a Romanesque church was built which was consecrated in 1147, completed towards 1164 and known by the name of Saint Stephen's from 1220 onwards.

The two west towers were immediately referred to as the "Pagan Towers", given that they were built with material taken from the "pagan" Roman camps. Later, the university of Vienna was established in the 13th century Bürgerschule (citizens' school), at Saint Stephen's.

The fire of 1258 in the reign of King Otakar of Bohemia, made substantial renovation works necessary. Most affected were the Pagan Towers, the west matronea, and the *Riesentor* (Door of the Giants, whose name probably derives from middle-high German, referring perhaps to the high pointed spires or to the gigantic mammoth bones, exhibited here at one time). From 1304 to 1340 the Albertine Choir was added to the basilica, (its name derives from Albert I),

but the present-day shape of the cathedral has not been modified since 1500, after a series of renovations in the Gothic style. In the central apse windows the remains of the original glass are still visible. The central choir has always been consecrated to Christ and to Saint Stephen, the north choir (or women's choir) to the Virgin (left), and the south choir to the Apostles (right).

With the construction of a collegiate abbey directed by a provost of princely rank, Rudolf the Founder succeeded in 1365 in freeing Vienna from the jurisdiction of the bishop of

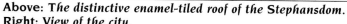
Above: *The distinctive enamel-tiled roof of the Stephansdom.*
Right: *View of the city.*

Passau - a very important move for the constitution of the diocese.

The Gothic nave was built in the form of a shell inside the Romanesque basilica: in this way masses could continue to be celebrated. The west facade was extended with the construction of two chapels, situated one on top of the other, next to both the towers.In 1426 the old inner church was demolished and in 1433 the majestic *Steffl* was completed, the "south tower", by Hans Prachatitz and Hans Puchsbaum, who followed the original designs by Michael Knabb, after the ambitious civic project to build an even higher tower was not carried out, owing to static diffi-culties; this project ended with the partial dismantling of the tower.

The works to the north tower - or *Adlerturm* (Eagle Tower) - got under-way in 1450. The presence of two towers was the symbol of a church of episcopal (or cathedral) type, and in fact the church did become a dio-cese shortly afterwards (1469). In 1523 the tower building works were suspended for aesthetic motives and the "trunk" was completed by Kaspar and Hans Saphoy with a mag-nificent dome in the years 1566-78. At the beginning of the 16th century Anton Pilgram was made responsi-ble, above all, for the cathedral inte-rior, where he executed works which made him immortal, such as the *Orgelfuss* (the organ base) in 1513 and the *Pilgramkanzel* (Pilgram pulpit) of 1514, both with his self-portrait. In 1945 the roof was destroyed by fire; the *Pummerin*, the bell which many years before had been moulded from the molten bronze of a Turkish cannon, fell from the Steffl and was smashed to smithereens. Priceless works of art were lost, but donations from all nine of the Bundesländer (Federal States) made reconstruc-tion possible. Even the Pummerin was recast at St. Florian (Upper Aus-tria) and each year, since 1952, it has rung in the New Year from the North Tower.

Interior of the Stephansdom.

TOUR OF THE INTERIOR

The cathedral is 107 m long and measures 70 m in width; the height of the side nave and the median are 22.4 m and 28 m respectively, while the choir reaches a height of 22.4 m.

The Door of the Giants (*Riesentor*) gives access to the cathedral's central nave.

NORTH-EAST CORNER (LEFT)

Here we can see the Chapel of the Crucifix (*Kreuzkapelle*) with the tomb of Prince Eugène of Savoy (1754) and a Christ on the cross, whose beard is made of real hair: the wooden crucifix dates back to the 15th century. The *Valentinskapelle* above is not open to visitors.

SOUTH-WEST CORNER (RIGHT)

Here we find the Chapel of Saint Elijah or Chapel of the Dukes (*Herzogskapelle*), with the altar of Saint Valentine of 1507 and the "House of the Mother of God" (14th century). The Royal Chapel (*Königskapelle*) at the higher level is not accessible.

LEFT-HAND SIDE NAVE
(AS FAR AS THE NORTH TOWER)

Along the way we can see the Altar of the Heart of Christ (*Herz-Jesu-Altar*), the Puchheim Canopy (*Puchheimbaldachin*, 1434), the *Franz-Seraph-Altar*, with an altar-piece by Michael Rottmayr of 1715 and the Altar of Francis Xavier (*Franz-Xaver-Altar*). The Altar of Saints Peter and Paul (*Peter und Paul Altar*), belonging to the Corporation of Stone-cutters, has an altar-piece by Tobias Pock of 1677. Next to the base which at one time housed the organ (*Orgelfuss*), we can see a self-portrait by Anton Pilgram.

NORTH TOWER

In the pronaos we find the Christ with toothache (*Zahnwehherrgott*), a bust of Christ suffering from 1425. It is said that some noble youths, punished for their blasphemous words with severe toothache, found relief only after showing remorse before the crucifix.

In the area next to the pronaos is the Chapel of Saint Barbara (*Barbarakapelle*).

MEDIAN NAVE, LEFT-HAND PILLARS (FROM THE BACK)

Here we find the Pilgram pulpit (*Pilgramkanzel*), a masterpiece by Anton Pilgram of 1514. The upper figures represent the four Fathers of the Church. On the base we can recognize the self-portrait of the master, known as the "onlooker at the window" (*Fenstergucker*). On the steps is a dog, the symbol of the preacher, which bars entry to various toads and lizards, symbols of evil. This unusual image represents a play on words: the preachers were often Dominicans (in Latin 'dominicanes'), which is why "Domini-canes" has been interpreted as "dogs of the Lord".
On the fourth pillar we can see the altar of Saint Catherine or of Saint Cecilia, while at the fifth pillar is the altar of "Mary in the Sun" of 1493.

MEDIAN NAVE, RIGHT-HAND PILLARS (FROM THE BACK)

At the third column we can see the Altar of Saint John the Baptist of 1708, while the Januarius Altar of 1711 stands at the fourth pillar. The Altar of Saint Joseph of 1699 stands at the fifth column.

RIGHT-HAND SIDE NAVE (AS FAR AS THE SOUTH TOWER)

Beneath a late Gothic canopy is the Altar of Maria Pócs with its unusual icon by the painter Stephan Pap (1676), famous for the miracle of the tears. Originating from Hungary, it was transported to Vienna in 1697 at the behest of Emperor Leopold I. Among the other altars worthy of mention are the altar of Saint Sebastian, the Altar of the Trinity (*Dreifaltigkeitsaltar*) and the altar of Leopold (*Leopoldsaltar*) beneath the *Füchselbaldachin*, by Hans Puchsbaum (1448).

SOUTH TOWER

Legend has it that a female servant wrongfully accused of theft, by praying fervently to the statue of the Madonna which we see here, was cleared of all the accusations: subsequently the statue (1320-30) came to be known as the Madonna of the Servant (*Dienstbotenmuttergottes*).
The heptagonal wooden cover of the

Above: the Gothic pulpit by Anton Pilgram.
Below: A detail of the pulpit. The busts of the four Fathers of the Church.

baptismal font by Ulrich Auer (1476) in the Chapel of Saint Catherine, was located, until the mid-20th century, above the *Pilgramskanzel* as a canopy.

NORTH NAVE (LEFT) OF THE ALBERTINE CHOIR

On the *Wiener-Neustätter-Altar*, brought here in 1884, are the symbolic initials of Emperor Frederick III, "AEIOU", whose real significance is unknown, notwithstanding the numerous attempts at interpretation. In the centre of the triptych we can see a Madonna and Child, flanked by Saint Barbara with the

Tower and Saint Catherine with the Sword. On the north wall is the marble sarcophagus of Rudolf the Founder.

MEDIAN NAVE OF THE ALBERTINE CHOIR

The Baroque High Altar of 1640-47 is made of marble and is the work of Johann Jakob Pock, while the altarpiece painted on tin and depicting the "stoning of Saint Stephen", is the work of his brother Tobias. The choir behind the altar in the median nave is divided from the altar of St. John of Nepomuk (side pillar on the

left, with an altar-piece by Kremser Schmidt) and from the altar of Saint Carlo Borromeo (right-hand pillar, with an altar-piece created using a particular technique for working the marble by Wolfgang Koepp in 1783).

SOUTH NAVE (RIGHT) OF THE ALBERTINE CHOIR

The tomb of Emperor Frederick III is a precious work made of Rotscheck marble and originating from Adnet. The tomb stone (1467, by Niklas Gerhaert van Leyden) shows the emperor in his official garments for the coronation; the 54 sacred scenes on the balustrade are by M. Tichter, while the "*Kaiserstiftungen*" (donations of the emperor) in relief, are the work of M. Valmet.

TOUR OF THE EXTERIOR WEST FACADE

The niches in the forepart contain both Romanesque figures, such as "Samson taming the lions" and the Griffin, and figures with a sixteenth-century historical subject, a "Judge" with his legs crossed, and "Saint Stephen". The first storey of the "Pagan Tower", 65 m high, is of the 12th century, whilst the present-day aspect dates back to 1500. In the relief on the gable of the *Riesentor* (1240), in late-Romanesque style, dominates a "Christ" inside a typical Gothic mandorla, with his knee bared as a sign of dominion. On the capitals are depictions of the Apostles and mythological animals.

NORTH AREA (LEFT)

The *Bischofstor* (Bishop's Door 1360-65) is preceded by a small hexagonal arcade where the visitor can observe events in the life of the Virgin Mary shown in relief. The Eagle Door (*Adlertor* in the North Tower) was not completed: building was totally suspended in 1523 and in 1566-78, Kaspar and Hans Savoy gave the trunk a Renaissance finish. We then come to the Capistrano Pulpit (*Kapistrankanzel*) in the corner of the north choir. In 1451 the Franciscan, Saint Giovanni Capistrano from Aquileia,

Detail of the Capistrano Pulpit: the statue which surmounts it depicts the Saint triumphing over the Turkish invader.

championed the crusade against the Turks from a wooden pulpit, whose stone copy is now surmounted by a high-relief depicting the "apotheosis of the Saint" (1737-38).

CENTRAL APSE OF THE CHOIR

There are three reliefs of the Passion (1420-30), a "Fresco of the poor souls" by Joseph Danhauser (1826) and other frescoes of the Passion of around 1500, located between the central apse and the south apse.

SOUTH AREA

Lackner's Prayer in the Garden (*Lackner'sche Oelberg*) is a relief of 1502 and the Straub Epitaph (*Straub'sche Epitaph*), depicting the "Leave-taking of Christ" and the "Seven Sorrows of the Virgin", of 1517, both reliefs in sandstone, were donations by the homonymous Fathers of the Church.

SOUTH TOWER, "STEFFL" (LITTLE STEPHEN)

The Steffl, 136.44 m high, was completed in 1433 by Hans Prachatitz according to the tradition of the Parlers, builders of the cathedral in Prague (*Veitsdom*). It should be observed that both towers, although not completely independent, are detached from the central body of the cathedral. The *Starhemberg-Bank* and the *Türmerstube* (72 m), served to watch enemy movements in 1683, during the Turkish occupation.

In the past a small prime bell ("*Prim*") invited the clergy to pass through the Door of the small prime bell (*Primglöckleintor*), thus entering the south tower, for morning prayers. The small hexagonal arcade of the Singers' Door (*Singertor*, 1360-65), an extremely valuable work in the Viennese Gothic style, is the work of Hans Puchsbaum (1440-50).

On the walls: figures of Rudolf the Founder and his consort Catherine of Bohemia. The relief on the gable represents the legend of Saint Paul. Next to the door: the tomb of Neithart Fuchs, a mediaeval singer of courtly love.

On the south arm of the transept rises the beautiful German Gothic bell-tower: the "Steffl".

GRABEN

(THE DITCH)
(1. district)

Towards 1200, during the enlargement of the city, the old ditch was uncovered which at one time protected the Roman legionary camp in the south-east area. It was turned into a square which has survived to the present day and is known as *Graben* (ditch). For many centuries this square was used as a food market, but gradually its appearance changed, and it acquired a much more elegant aspect, as was fitting, and it was used as the setting for great religious and courtly festivals. The entire complex of the square is today dominated by buildings with facades in the Jugendstil (floral style) or Neo-classical style, whilst only in the lanes does the Baroque style still survive.

The centre of Graben is embodied by the *Dreifaltigkeitssäule*, the "Column of the Trinity" (consecrated in 1692), together with the two fountains, the *Josefsbrunnen* to the west and the *Leopoldsbrunnen* to the east, which in relief recounts the legend of the foundation of the monastery of Neuburg, the work of Saint Leopold.

The column owes its origin to a prayer of thanks which Emperor Leopold I gave up for the end of the plague of 1679; it is for this reason that it is still called "*Pestsäule*" (Plague Column). The original wooden column was to have been replaced by M. Rauchmiller with a marble column, but the project was deferred due to the Turkish war of 1683 and Ludovico O. Burnacini and Johann Bernh Fischer von Erlach received the commission to design a new column, using the pedestals and the three figures of angels already existing. The relief is the work of Ignaz Bendl, the putti were created by Rauchmiller and others, including Paul Strudel, who in addition designed the group of the Trinity (executed in gilded copper by Johann. Kilian, Augsburg).

Graben: **the plague column.**

PETERSKIRCHE

(CHURCH OF SAINT PETER)
(St. Peter's Square, 1)

It is said that in 792 Charlemagne stayed in this area to defend himself from the threat of the Avars, who came from the east, and that he founded a church here on the stones of a holy Roman building of the 4th century. The marble relief by Rudolf Weyr (1906), on the external part of the Church of Saint Peter, refers to these events, which are not historically documented.

The present-day form of the church dates back to designs by G. Montani, substantially modified by Lukas von Hildebrandt. In 1708 Hildebrandt completed the first construction, and in 1733 the two, relatively low, leaning towers were erected, which lend the concave facade a dynamic appearance, integrating it effectively into the majestic spaces of the ancient city.

The best Austrian artists of the Baroque contributed to the creation of the church's interior, including the most famous painters of the 19th century (L. Kupelwieser and J. Fürich). The central dome is characterized by the fresco of the "Annunciation of the Virgin" or "The Assumption" by Johan Michael Rottmayr (1714). The altar-piece on the High Altar, executed by S. Bussi to a design by Galli-Bibiena, shows "The Healing of the Paralytic", the work of Martin Altomonte. On the beautiful tabernacle we find the "Immaculate Mary" by Kupelwieser. At the end of the Choir we can see the pulpit by Matthias Steinl (1716), and opposite it a highly dramatic work, the "Fall of Saint John of Nepomuk into the Vltava River", a gilded wooden group of 1729, the work of Lorenzo Mattielli. The six Side Altars and the altars in the Choir are the work of Rottmayr, M. Altomonte, Schoonjans, Johann G. Schmidt, Kupelwieser, Führich and others. On the forepart of the portal (1753) by Andrea Altomonte, are some leaden figures, created by the pupil of Donner Franz Kohl: they represent various angels with the papal insignia and "Faith", "Hope" and "Love".

VERMÄHLUNGSBRUNNEN

(THE NUPTIAL FOUNTAIN)
(1, Hoher Markt)

In 1702 Emperor Leopold I solemnly promised that if his son Joseph I should return safely from the war, he would erect a column to Saint Joseph. Charles VI had the project replaced with a marble fountain designed by J.E. Fischer von Erlach and executed by A. Corradini, depicting the holy nuptial group showing Joseph, Mary and various prelates. A canopy in bronze crowned with a representation of the Trinity rises above the group.

ANKERUHR

(THE ANKER CLOCK)

(1, Hoher Markt)

In 1913 the painter Franz von Matsch placed an artistic clock in the Jugendstil on the Gothic arch of the Anker insurance company (Hoher Markt 10), at number 11 of the building.
Thanks to its special mechanism, each day at the strike of noon, various statues which represent important Austrian historical personages file past to the sound of music.

Above: *Two buildings overlook the square, joined by a bronze and copper clock, known as Ankeruhr.*
Right: *In the middle of the oldest square in Vienna, Hoher Markt, stands the Nuptial Fountain.*

ALTES RATHAUS

(OLD TOWN HALL)
(1, Wipplingerstrasse 8)

Notwithstanding the numerous reconstructions which took place up until the 18th century, the old town hall has a mediaeval nucleus. Both the portals of the Baroque facade created between 1699 and 1706 by J. Martin Fischer, are decorated with allegorical figures: on the first "Justice" and "Goodness", on the second "Devotion" and "Faith".

The plaster vaults of the impressive Great Hall are by Albrecht Carmesina (1712-13). Raphael Donner designed the "Andromeda-brunnen" (Andromeda fountain - 1741) in the inner courtyard. When the New Town Hall was built on the Ring in 1883, the building lost its original function. Nowadays it is the headquarters of the district management and the documentation archive of the Austrian Resistance (Staircase III).

MARIA AM GESTADE

(CHURCH OF MARIA ON THE RIVER BANK)
(Maria Stiegen; 1, Salvatorgasse 12)

The name itself of the church indicates that in ancient times it stood on the bank of an old arm of the Danube and on the ditch of a legionary camp and was built on the main Roman walls, rising up majestically on the steep slope of the ancient city.

This ancient church of the Virgin was officially documented in 1158. The Romanesque church was destroyed by fire in 1262, and for this reason, in the 14th century, a sumptuous new construction was built. Its noble, narrow western facade, its polygonal bell-tower, 56 m high, with the fine filigree dome by Michael Knab, circa 1430, provide, together with the 14th and 15th century windows, the most representative evidence of Gothic Vienna remaining today. On the right-hand part of the nave is the tomb of the Patron Saint of the city, St. Klemens Maria Hofbauer (1758-1820).

The Old Civilian Arsenal.

BÜRGERLICHES ZEUGHAUS

(OLD CIVILIAN ARSENAL)
(1, Am Hof 10)

Until the end of the 19th century, arms and trophies were housed in this building, reconstructed in 1732 in the Baroque style by Anton Ospel after the destruction which took place during the Turkish invasion, and embellished by Lorenzo Mattielli with elegant decorations on the pediment. After 1848, the year in which it was discovered to be only too easy for revolutionaries to take up arms, a "fortress" arsenal was built in the third district to avoid a repetition of what had happened in the past. The Fire Brigade station is now located in what used to be the arsenal.

SCHOTTENKLOSTER

(MONASTERY OF THE SCOTS)
(1, Freyung Square)

Its name derives from the Irish monks, summoned to Vienna in 1155 by Henry II, and erroneously called "Scottish".

Afterwards, in 1418, the Benedictines established themselves here, and gave the church the name of "Our Lady of the Scots" (the oldest image of the Virgin Mary in Vienna is worshipped here, dating back to around 1250 and placed on the altar in the left transept). From 1643-48 the church was given its present-day Baroque form. The facade of the Scottish convent is by J. Kornhäusel, the greatest architect of the Biedermeier style. In the crypt lie Henry II, the founder of the church, and Count Starhemberg, defender of Vienna in 1683. Also of noteworthy importance is the convent's *Gemäldegalerie* (picture gallery). We would like to point out the Altar of the Master of the Scots (*Schottenmeister-Altar*), with its nineteen Gothic panels.

KIRCHE AM HOF

(OR CHURCH OF THE "NINE ANGELIC CHOIRS")
(1, Am Hof)

The Am Hof Square takes its name from the Palatinate of the Babenbergers, who originated from here. In 1386-1403 the Carmelites built a Gothic church in place of the Palatinate chapel, which in 1554 was given to the Jesuits, summoned to Vienna to implement the Counter-Reformation.

After the Baroque adaptations to the interior (1610), Carlo Antonio Carlone, in 1662, gave the church a new facade. In 1782, from the balcony of the *Marienkirche* (church of the Virgin Mary or "of the Nine Angelic Choirs"), Pope Pius VI, who had come to Vienna to mitigate Joseph II's anti-clerical reforms, gave the Easter blessing. It was in this same place that Emperor Francis I announced his coronation as Austrian Emperor in 1804 and it was here that in 1806 he relinquished the German crown.

The Schottenkirche is characterized by its sober Neo-classical facade and its sumptuous Baroque interior.
The fourteenth-century church of the Nine Angelic Choirs.

RINGSTRASSE

(RINGROAD)

On 20th December 1857 Emperor Francis Joseph I gave permission for the bastions and the fortifications which surrounded the inner city to be demolished, so that the surrounding open areas, the so-called Glacis, could be made use of. It is thus that space was made for the creation of what today is known as the Ringstrasse. The frenetic building activity which followed gave the entire age the name of the "Ringstrasse Epoch", whilst "Ringstrasse Style" has become an architectural term. Along the grandiose new street, government buildings, the Votive Church, theatres, the Opera House, museums, concert halls and a series of elegant town houses for private use were constructed. In addition to the idea of a four-lane road which could run alongside the above-mentioned buildings, the aim was to replace the unused green area of the Glacis by opening up and enlarging parks.

BÖRSE

(THE STOCK EXCHANGE)
(1, Schottenring 16)

The Viennese Stock Exchange building, constructed by Theophil Hansen in the Neo-Renaissance style in 1874-77, was totally destroyed by fire. It was E. Boltestern who was made responsible for its restoration, and in 1959 the building was reopened. The large Stock Exchange Hall, which had been completely destroyed together with its precious ceiling, could not, however, be salvaged and it was transformed into an inner courtyard, with characteristic greenish walls.

VOTIVKIRCHE

(THE VOTIVE CHURCH)
(9, Rooseveltplatz)

In 1853 Emperor Francis Joseph had escaped almost unscathed from a failed assassination attempt by the Hungarian Libenyi. In order to give thanks, his brother, Archduke Maximilian commissioned the construction

of the Church of the "Vow" of Our Lord the Redeemer. In 1863 Maximilian allowed himself to be persuaded by the French Emperor Napoleon III to take the crown of Mexico, but on the 19th June 1867 he was murdered in Querétaro, by order of Benito Juarez. The Votive Church was built in 1856-79 by Heinrich Ferstel on the model of the French Gothic cathe-

drals. It has three naves and two towers 99 m high. In the chapel containing the baptismal font we find the tomb of Count Niklas Salm who in 1529 defended Vienna from the Turks: it is the work of L. Hering and dates back to around 1533.

To the right of the High Altar is the Flemish "Altar of Antwerp" of the 15th century.

Below: *The facade of the Votivkirche, characterized by its soaring openwork spires.*
Right-hand page: *Detail of the facade.*

NEUE UNIVERSITÄT

(THE NEW UNIVERSITY)
(1, Dr.-Karl-Lueger-Ring 1)

It was erected in 1873-83 by Heinrich Ferstel who, out of the Alma Mater Rudolfina, put up a new building in the Italian Renaissance style. It is the oldest German-speaking university, given that the one in Prague can no longer be considered as German, and was founded in 1365 by Rudolf the Founder.

BURGTHEATER

(COURT THEATRE)
(1, Dr.-Karl-Lueger-Ring 2)

Joseph II had transformed the theatre in the Michaelerplatz into the German National Theatre. When the latter had to make way for the Ringstrasse and the Imperial Palace, it was replaced by the new Imperial Court Theatre, known as the *Burg* (1874-1888).

Gottfried Semper was commissioned to design the external structure and Carl Hasenauer the decora-

Above: *The University lies on the Ring.*
Below: *The Burgtheater.*

tion of the interiors; both took Italian Renaissance art for their model. The work of Semper reveals the influence of the art of Dresden.

The top floor of the central building is decorated with a bas-relief 18 m long, the B*acchantenzug* (Procession of Bacchus) by Rudolf Weyr. For the balustrade which surmounts it, Carl Kundmann created the group representing "Apollo with the muses Melpomene (tragedy) and Thalia (comedy)". The paintings on the ceiling of the staircase in the side wings are the work of Franz von Matsch, Ernst and Gustav Klimt, who at that time worked together in the *Künstlerkompanie* (Company of Artists). The Burgtheater is still today one of the most important drama theatres in the German language.

Above: *The interior of the old* **Burgtheater in a painting by Gustav Klimt.**
Below: A *view of the main staircase.*

VOLKSGARTEN

(Public Garden)

In 1809, on their return to their homeland, the French troops had blown up the bastions in front of the Imperial palace. The latter was not rebuilt and on the newly-vacated area two gardens were created: the *Burg* or *Kaisergarten*, the imperial garden now lying between the new Imperial Palace and the Opera House, and the *Volksgarten* or public garden, which then, as now, was open to all alike and lies between the court theatre and the Heldenplatz (Heroes Square).

The Temple of Theseus, an imitation of the Theseion in Athens, created by P. Nobile in 1823, originally housed the sculpture depicting "Theseus' struggle with the centaurs" by Antonio Canova (now in the Foyer of the *Kunsthistorisches Museum* - History of Art Museum).

The monument to the Empress Elizabeth by Hans Bitterlich (1907) recalls her tragic death in the assasination attempt at Geneva in 1898.

A *view from the Volksgarten with the Burgtheater in the background.*
Bottom left: *Monument to Empress Elizabeth, assassinated in 1898 in Geneva.*
Bottom right: *The Temple of Theseus.*

NEUES RATHAUS

(NEW TOWN HALL)
(1, Rathausplatz)

The grandiose and solemn town hall building, built in 1872-73 by Friedrich Schmidt, inspired by Neo-Gothic forms, is separated from the Ring by the park in front, which maximizes to a remarkable extent its massive, impressive facade.

At the top of the central tower, 98 m high, is the "*Rathausmann*", a statue more than three metres high by Alexander Nehr, an imitation of an equestrian statue of the Emperor Maximilian I belonging to the weaponry collection in the *Neue Burg*, which for a long time has been one of the symbols of Vienna. During the summer, in the town hall's *Arkadenhof* (arcade courtyard), the so-called "Arcade Concerts" are held. In addition it is possible to go on a guided tour of the Private Room of the Mayor and the Municipal Council.

The New Town Hall, where the Municipal and Provincial Assembly of Vienna has its headquarters.

PARLAMENT

(PARLIAMENT)
(1, Dr.-Karl-Renner-Ring 3)

The building of the *Reichsrat* (council of the Reich), belonging to the Austrian-Hungarian monarchy, is a masterpiece by Theophil Hansen, and was created in 1874-83. Since 1918 the Parliament has been the headquarters of the National Council and the *Bundesrat* (Federal Council) of the Austrian Republic.

The external architectural style shows the clear influence of ancient Greek art. An impressive double ramp leads to the arcade, passing alongside marble statues of famous personages, and is flanked by bronze statues depicting horse-breakers. The "goddess of wisdom", the main figure of the *Pallas - Athene Brunnen* (fountain of Pallas-Athena), is the work of Carl Kundmann (1902). At the feet of the goddess we find the most important personages of the Imperial House. The allegorical figures *"Gesetzgebende"* (Legislative Power) and *"Ausübende*

Gewalt" (Executive Power) are the work of J. Tautenhayn.

The relief on the pediment in the pronaos represents the "Granting of the Constitution to the Austrian people by Francis Joseph in 1861" (Edmund Hellmer). In 1905, in front of the peristyle, decorated with mo-

saics, a monument was erected to Theophil von Hansen, the builder of Parliament (bronze bust by Haerdtl). The two long side buildings on either side of the central body, end in two small, slightly protruding, angular, temple-style pavilions. The Sittings Halls (*Sitzungssäle*)

The Parliament, with the chambers of the Nationalrat (National Council) and the Bundesrat (Federal Council).

Top: *the Museum Quarter.*
Bottom left: *the Leopold Museum.* Bottom right: *the* MUMOK (*Museum of Modern Art Ludwig Foundation of Vienna*).

in the Parliament, situated in both the rear buildings, are characterized by the bronze monument of Eight Triumphal Chariots with four horses (quadrigae).

MUSEUMSQUARTIER WIEN

(VIENNA'S NEW MUSEUM QUARTER)

Right across from the traditional Viennese museums, on an area of 60,000 square meters, there now arises a true city within a city—with a cultural vocation. Modern architecture stands in harmony with the traditional to give life to a new complex that forms a single aggregate with the Imperial Palace, the Neue Burg, and the Kunsthis-torisches and Naturhistorisches Museums.

In 1713, Emperor Karl VI entrusted Johann Bernhard Fischer von Erlach with construction of a new building for the imperial stables. From 1921 onward, the building was the milieu for exhibitions and trade fairs. In 1985, the Exhibition Palace (Messepalast) became the central venue of the Vienna Music Festival. But the idea of creating a cultural center was hatched earlier, in 1980, and by 2001 the new Museum Quarter was a reality. The particular infrastructures, the enclosed courtyards, and the gardens all unite to lend this complex a feeling of great uniformity—although it offers something for everyone.

Leopold Museum. Among its many vaunts, this museum of modern Austrian art—the most important of its kind—hosts the world's largest collection of works by Egon Schiele.

MUMOK (Museum of Modern Art Ludwig Foundation of Vienna). This museum houses one of Europe's most extensive collections of modern and contemporary art.

Kunsthalle Wien. In essence, this is a center for international contemporary art, where the most important Austrian works dated 1945 and later are displayed. The *Veranstaltungshallen der Gemeinde Wien* (City of Vienna Exhibition Hall Center) hosts the *Tanzquartier* (Dance Quarter), the *Tabakmuseum*

Above: *an aerial view of the Museumsquartier or Museum Quarter, with the Kunsthistorisches and Naturhistorisches Museums in the foreground.*

(Museum of Tobacco), the *Architekturzentrum Wien* (Architectural Center of Vienna), the *Theaterhaus für Kinder* (Children's Theater), and other attractions.

What is more, these halls are still the headquarters of the Vienna Music Festival.

"Vienna-District 21" (in the buildings originally built by the Fischer von Erlachs) is instead a workplace used regularly by artists and researchers.

The elegant square dedicated to Empress Maria Theresa, flanked by the Kunsthistorisches and Naturhistorisches Museums.

KUNSTHISTORISCHES & NATURHISTORISCHES MUSEUM

(HISTORY OF ART MUSEUM AND NATURAL SCIENCE MUSEUM)
(Burgring 5 and 7 respectively)
The two museums, standing one opposite the other, close off Maria Theresa Square, the empress to whom the monument by Caspar Zumbusch and Carl Hasenauer is dedicated. The former was responsible for the statues, the latter for the architectural design. The statue of the empress enthroned is surround-ed by equestrian statues of her generals and by statues of her councillors. In the reliefs on the gables great personalities such as Mozart, Haydn and Gluck are recorded. The two mirror-like buildings (Gottfried Semper 1872-88; creation of the interiors: Hasenauer) are distinguished by the statues of the two facades: on the former we find allegorical figures and masters of art, on the latter allegories of natural forces.

On the ceiling of the staircase of the *Kunsthistorisches Museum*, we can see "The apotheosis of art", by Munkácsy. The 12 lunette paintings by Hans Makart, which represent great painters and their favourite subjects, as well as the 40 mosaic pictures by F. Matsch, Ernst and Gustav Klimt, clearly demonstrate that in the construction of the interior no expense was spared. The marble group by Canova, "Theseus' struggle with the

centaurs", was previously in the Temple of Theseus in the Volksgarten. The museum contains a collection of Egyptian antiquities and, in addition, objects which date back to the ancient Greek, Etruscan and early Christian periods, up until the early Middle Ages, a collection of plastic and decorative art, a highly-renowned picture gallery with works by Titian, Tintoretto, Raphael, Caravaggio, Tiepolo, Velasquez, Rembrandt, Bosch and many others, as well as the largest collection of the works of Pieter Breughel the Elder, a coin collection and the Ambraser portrait collection. In the *Naturhistorisches Museum* the ceiling painting above the staircase is by Hans Canon and represents "The cycle of life". The private collections of Emperor Francis I, consort of Maria Theresa, constituted the basis of the museum, which later on, under Francis Joseph I, was to be remarkably enriched and enlarged. It houses mineralogical, petrographic, geological, paleontological, prehistoric, anthropological, zoological and botanical collections. The whole is completed by a *Kindersaal* (Children's Room).

Interiors of the Museum - **above:** *the sculpted group by Canova, Theseus slaying the Minotaur.*

The salt-cellar by B. Cellini. It represents the union between the Sea and the Earth.

Rubens - "The four corners of the earth", the four women representing the continents are flanked by powerful figures of river gods.

On this page:
above:
*Diego Velazquez -
"The Infanta
Margaret Theresa,
aged eight, dressed
in blue".*

below:
*Breughel the Elder
- "Return of the
hunters".*

Page 35:
*Raphael -
"Madonna and
Child".*

Pages 36-37:
*Breughel the Elder
- "The wedding
feast".*

STAATSOPER

(OPERA HOUSE)
(1, Opernring 2)

The Opera House was built in 1862 and was the first building constructed in the Ring. The architects, August von Siccardsburg and Eduard van der Nüll created the Opera House in the French Renaissance style but were bitterly criticised. The rejection of their work led van der Nüll to commit suicide and caused the death from a heart attack of Siccardsburg. When the Opera House was opened in 1869 with Mozart's "Don Giovanni", the two architects were already dead. In the open colonnades of the two-storey loggia which looks onto the Ringstrasse, we find five statues in bronze by Ernst J. Hähnel. These represent Heroism, Drama, Imagination, Comedy and Love. The "Frescos of the magic flute" in the loggia are the work of Moritz von Schwind. The bust of Mahler in the Foyer, is the work of Rodin.

Following a bombardment in 1945 the theatre was completely destroyed by flames. The reconstruction lasted ten years: Erich Boltenstern designed the stalls and the staircases whilst Zeno Kosak designed the hall.

Above: *Detail of one of the two twin fountains standing either side of the Opera House.*
Below: *Facade of the State Opera House.*

The iron curtain depicting Orpheus and Eurydice is the work of Rudolf Eisenmenger. On 5th November 1955 the Opera House was re-opened, in a solemn ceremony, and a performance of Beethoven's "Fidelio" was given, conducted by Karl Böhm. The opera orchestra is made up of members of the Vienna Philharmonic Orchestra. In addition it has its own State Opera House Corps de Ballet. A list of its orchestra conductors alone would be enough to attest to its worldwide reputation: Gustav Mahler, Richard Strauss, Furtwängler, Böhm, Herbert von Karajan, Maazel and Abbado.

Right: *A glimpse of the staircase decorated with statues of the nine muses by Joseph Gasser.*
Below: *The entrance with the double staircase which leads to the boxes.*

KÄRNTNERSTRASSE

If you follow the Ring round to the junction of the Opera House with Kärntnerstrasse, you will be unable to resist the lure of this street. It is not just the exclusive shops and their window displays which attract attention: especially in summer, the visitor will be surprised and charmed by the excellent "street music" (often performed by the students of the nearby Music Academy), or by the impromptu stunts and acrobatics of its street artists.

Kärntnerstrasse.

STADTPARK

(CITY PARK)
(1, Parkring)

The park was designed in 1862-63 during the construction of the Ring. In 1906 Friedrich Ohmann was made responsible for the architecture of the entrance, next to the tram stop, and together with J. Hackhofer created the Pavilions near the Wien water course, which crosses the park. The monument to Franz Schubert (C. Kundmann, T. Hansen; 1872) is a donation from the *Männergesang-Verein* (male choir) of Vienna. In 1797, Schubert, known as the "Liederfürst" (prince of *Lieder*), was born in the house in Nussdorferstrasse 54 (now a Muse-

um). He was the pupil of Salieri, that master of the court orchestra who according to unfounded rumour, from Puschkin to the present-day, was supposed to have poisoned Mozart. But "Schwammerl", the nickname by which his friends called him, died all too soon (1828): he will always be remembered as a Maestro both of the Lieder genre as well as of symphony music.

Another immortal Viennese, the "King of the waltz" Johann Strauss (1825-99), had a bronze monument with an arch in relief dedicated to him (E. Helmer, 1921). Strauss probably once played in the Kursalon here, inaugurated in 1867 and used ever since as a venue for "light" music, such as the waltz or operetta.

REGIERUNGSGEBÄUDE

(GOVERNMENT BUILDING)
(1, Stubenring 1)

The building, erected in 1909-13, was the War Ministry and is nowadays the headquarters of various ministries. The monument dedicated to Marshal Radetzky by C. Zumbusch, 1892, until 1912 was in the Ministry of War in the Am Hof Square.

ÖSTERREICHISCHES MUSEUM FÜR ANGEWANDTE KUNST

(AUSTRIAN MUSEUM OF APPLIED ARTS)
(1, Stubenring 5)

In 1871 the collection of the Art and Industry Museum was housed in this building, built by Heinrich Ferstel. Near the wall which divides the museum from the university of Applied Art, we find the *Pallas-Athene Brunnen* (Pallas-Athena fountain) decorated with a mosaic by Ferdinand Laufberger, whilst the architectural structure is the work of Heinrich Ferstel.

This building, whose mosaic represents the Five Continents, and is the work of Eduard Veith, stands on Kärntnerstrasse.

Stadtpark, the monument to Johann Strauss.

HOFBURG

(IMPERIAL PALACE)

The Imperial Palace, represents, with its 18 wings, 54 staircases, 19 courtyards and around 2,600 rooms, the real centre of the Austrian sovereigns' secular power. It was the residence from 1439 to 1806 of the Romanic and German kings and emperors, whilst from 1804 to 1918 the Austrian emperors resided there.

It was the tradition that no sovereign should live in the rooms inhabited by his predecessor; for this reason the series of enlargements carried out has given to the whole an extremely heterogeneous character, notwithstanding the various attempts to construct a harmonious and uniform complex.

The buildings of the imperial residence, which shows a deeply European character, date back to various epochs: from the "neue" Burg of the Babenbergers, to the Wehrburg of Otakar of Bohemia and the Neue Burg of the Ringstrasse epoch.

HELDENPLATZ

(HEROES SQUARE)

Coming from the Ring, we now go through the *Äussere Burgtor* (external door of the palace). The Neue Burg is on the right, further on we find the *Heldenplatz*, and behind it the *Leopoldinische Trakt* (Leopold Wing), with the President of the Republic's offices. The French troops, when retreating, blew up the ancient *Burgtor* (the building's main door), dating from the Leopoldine epoch, as well as the bastion. A square was created with the demolition of the remains of the fortress, and was called Heldenplatz, "Heroes Square", after the inauguration of the equestrian statues of Prince Eugène of Savoy, the great general who defeated the Turks, and Archduke Charles, the general who defeated Napoleon at Aspern in 1809. The two monuments are by Dominik Fernkorn and date back to 1865 and 1860 respectively. Opposite the Hofburg (Imperial Palace) the square is delimited by the *Neue Tor* (New Door, 1821-24). In 1933 this became the Monument to the Fallen of the First World War. Since 1945 the Door has provided a space for the commemoration of the Fallen for the Freedom of Austria during the Nazi period.

Below: *View of the Heldenplatz, with the monument to Archduke Charles.*
Right-hand page: *Neue Burg, statue of Prince Eugène.*

NEUE HOFBURG

(NEW IMPERIAL PALACE)

The initial project by Gottfried Semper to create an "Imperial Forum" which, as well as constituting a mirror-like wing of the present-day New Imperial Palace, would be linked by a triumphal arch (above the Ring) to the museums opposite, was not carried out in its entirety. Semper collaborated on the construction of the New Imperial Palace (from 1879 to 1908) with Karl Hasenauer, Emil Förster, Friedrich Ohmann and towards the end Ludwig Baumann. Looking out onto Heroes Square, the building has a concave facade of grandiose proportions, whose upper floor is characterized by columns. It is the headquarters of several sections of the National Library, of a collection of weapons and of an important collection of antique musical instruments of the Kunsthistorisches Museum. Since 1978 it has housed the museum of Ephesus, given that, from the outset, Austrian archaeologists played a fundamental role in the excavations of ancient Ephesus; finally, in the Corps de Logis (wing towards the Ring) we find the *Völkerkunde-Museum* (Ethnographical Museum), and a part of the weapons collection.

Above: *Neue Hofburg.*
Below: *The Schweizertor, a 16th century door which leads to the oldest part of the Hofburg.*
Right-hand page:
above: *The Swiss Courtyard.*
below: *Plaque with the insignia of Emperor Ferdinand I.*

SCHWEIZERHOF

(Swiss Courtyard)
(Alte Burg) (Old Castle)

On entering the Door of the Leopold wing, the visitor arrives at the In der Burg square. On the right is the Swiss Courtyard, the oldest part of the castle; opposite the *Leopoldinischer Trakt* (Leopold Wing), we find the *Reichskanzleitrakt* (Imperial Chancellery). Finally the square is delimited by the *Amalienburg* (castle of Amalia). The *Schweizerhof* represents the nucleus of the complex of the old mediaeval castle, at one time protected by its four corner towers. The impressive *Schweizertor* (Swiss Door) leads to the inner courtyard. An inscription cites Ferdinand I as "the founder" (1552): Ferdinand, king of the Romans, of the Germans, the Hungarians, the Bohemians, etc., Infante of Spain, Archduke of Austria, Duke of Burgundy, etc. Anno MDLII (1552). The name, which was given to the whole wing, is due to the Swiss guards in the service of the Empress Maria

Theresa. The courtyard leads to the *Hofburgkapelle* (Imperial Chapel) and the *Schatzkammer* (Rooms of the Imperial Treasure). The *Hofburgkapelle* (the Imperial Chapel dedicated to the Assumption of the Virgin), was erected under Emperor Frederick III (1447-49). Subsequently it assumed a Baroque style and was enriched with neo-Gothic details, as can be seen in the pulpit. The 13 wooden figures on the pillars (1470-80) have now been attributed to Gerhaert van Leydens, author, besides, of the tomb of Frederick II, which is in the Cathedral. Every Sunday and on feast days, solemn masses are celebrated in the chapel with the participation of the *Wiener Sängerknaben* (Vienna Boys Choir) and the members of the Vienna Philharmonic.

The rooms of the *Schatzkammer*, unrivalled for their splendour and magnificence, draw their origins from the *Kunstkammer* (art rooms) founded in 1533 by Emperor Ferdinand I, and in time were constantly enlarged. The complex lock of the entrance door bears the initials of Emperor Charles VI who deposited his treasures here in 1712. The most precious pieces in the profane section are the Imperial Crown of the Holy Roman Empire, the Imperial Austrian Crown and the robes of the Order of the Golden Fleece, the order of the House of the Habsburgs. In the sacred section we should mention the treasure of the Hofburg Chapel and the Relics of the Imperial Crypt.

Crown of the Holy Roman Empire (962).

REICHSKANZLEITRAKT

(IMPERIAL CHANCELLERY)

The building was constructed by Hildebrandt and J.E. Fischer v. Erlach between 1723 and 1730 and was at one time the headquarters of the Imperial Council, the principal authority of the Holy Roman Empire; the sculptures outside the portals are by L. Mattielli.

The imperial apartments of Emperor Francis Joseph and the representative Audience Room, as well as the rooms in which the Duke of Reichstadt lived, are considered the most interesting parts of the wing.

AMALIENBURG

(CASTLE OF AMALIA)

The name dates back to the early 18th century, when the widow of Emperor Joseph I, Wilhelmine Amalia, lived in this castle. Construction works began at the time of Emperor Rudolf II, in circa 1575. Czar Alexander lived here during the Congress of Vienna and later on Empress Elizabeth lived in the apartments of the *Amalienburg*. The tower of the wing is decorated with a sundial with a quadrant showing the phases of the moon.

Above: *The Imperial Chancellery.*
Below: *The internal court known as "In der Burg" with the statue of Emperor Francis I, and in the background the Castle of Amalia distinguished by its beautiful Baroque tower decorated with a sundial.*

LEOPOLDINISCHER TRAKT

(LEOPOLDINE WING)

Erected by Filiberto Lucchesi in 1660-66 under Emperor Leopold I and rebuilt by Domenico Carlone in 1681 after a fire, the wing contains the rooms and ceremonial halls of Maria Theresa and her consort, Emperor Francis Stephen I. Although the empress preferred Schönbrunn, the interiors are highly representative just the same. Together with the apartment belonging to Josef II, since 1946 these rooms have been the headquarters of the Austrian Head of State's offices.

In the building which leads to the old castle are the Great Ceremonial Hall and the *Geheime Ratsstube* (Hall of the Secret Council), which since 1958 have been used by the Conference Centre of the Imperial Palace.

The imperial rooms can be visited with a Guide. The *Hoftafel- und Silberkammer* (Court dining-room and Silver room) contains various dinner services of the Imperial House of extraordinary value: for example the so-called "table triumph of Milan" or the "Vermeil Service" (in gold-plated silver, with 140 place-settings).

Back in the *In der Burg* (In the Court) Square, let us turn our attention to the impressive monument of Emperor Franz I, by Pompeo Marchesi. The day the first stone of this monument was put in place was the 18th October 1843, the anniversary of the battle of nations in Leipzig; it was Emperor Ferdinand I who chose that date to commemorate his father, who had played an important role in the defeat of Napoleon. This explains why the emperor is represented here as Emperor Augustus, in a particularly regal pose. The inscription on the plinth 'Amorem meum populis meis' means "my love to my peoples".

Above: *Banqueting hall.*
Below: *Audience chamber.*

Francis Joseph I in the formal uniform of an Austrian marshal.
Oil painting by Franz Xaver Winterhalter, 1865.

Elizabeth of Austria (Sissy)
Oil painting by Franz Xaver Winterhalter, 1865.

Francis Joseph I, Emperor of Austria, King of Hungary, born on 18th August 1830 in Vienna at the castle of Schönbrunn, son of Archduke Francis Charles and of Sophie, Princess of Bavaria, descendant of Emperor Francis II. He ascended to the throne after the abdication of his uncle Ferdinand I on 2nd December 1848. The emperor suffered much personal tribulation: the shooting of his brother Maximilian (Emperor of Mexico). The suicide of his only son Rudolf. The assassination of his wife Elizabeth and of his successor to the throne Francis Ferdinand (28.6.1914 in Sarajevo).

Elizabeth, Empress of Austria, Queen of Hungary, born on 24th December 1837 in Munich, Bavaria, daughter of Duke Maximilian of Bavaria and Duchess Ludovica. On 10th September 1898 she was stabbed by an anarchist in Geneva, Switzerland.

Their marriage took place on 24th April 1854 in the Augustinerkirche in Vienna.

MICHAELERTRAKT E MICHAELERPLATZ

(THE SAINT MICHAEL WING AND THE SQUARE OF SAINT MICHAEL)

Passing from the Imperial Square, through the Imperial Chancellery Door, to the Square of Saint Michael, we reach the *Oktogon*, the octagonal spired bell-tower in a wing of Saint Michael, a construction of the *Ringstrasse* epoch (Kirschner, 1893) which links the Imperial Chancellery with the Riding School.

The decorations on the portal of the facade which overlooks the Square of Saint Michael continue the theme of "Hercules", a theme which we find again in the part overlooking the *Burghof* (imperial courtyard). In the niches at the corners of the building are two monumental fountains which represent the allegorical figures of *Macht zur Lande* ("Earthly Dominion", E. Helmer 1897) and *Macht zur See* ("Maritime Dominion", R. Weyr 1895).

MICHAELERKIRCHE

The *Michaelerkirche* (church of Saint Michael), the second Parish Church of the city of Vienna, which until 1784 was the Court Parish Church, was built toward the mid-13th century. Its present form dates back to 1792, when E. Koch created its facade in the Neo-classical style.

The motif of the "Fall of the rebel angels" is developed in the sandstone group by Mattielli, on the forepart of the portal, in the colossal painting by Michelangelo Unterberger in the right-hand transept, and in the relief in the choir by Karl Georg Merville and lastly, on the High Altar (1781 - J.B. d'Avrange) with the icon of the *Wegweiserin Maria*

Above and Right-hand page: *Michaelertrakt*.
Below: The *Michaelerkirche*.

(Our Lady Help of Christians) originating from the isle of Crete, which at one time was fervently worshipped in Vienna. In the crypt of the Church of Saint Michael lie many noble personages, including the famous librettist of Mozart and master of Maria Theresa, P. Metastasio.

THE LOOSHAUS

The *Looshaus* (Michaelerplatz 5), erected in 1910 by Adolf Loos for the men's clothing company Goldman and Salatsch, earned the disapproval of the Viennese and their emperor, particularly due to the style of its *"augenbrauenlos"* windows (eyebrowless, i.e. without frames), but notwithstanding, Adolf Loos was one of the precursors of the subsequent most modern and linear architectural style. If we turn right out of the Square of Saint Michael into *Reitschulgasse* (Riding School lane), in the direction of the *Josephplatz* (Joseph Square), we come, on the left, to the *Stallburg* (Imperial Stable) and on the right to the *Winterreitschule* (Winter Riding School).

Above: *Spanish Riding School.*
Below: *The Looshaus, a building designed by Adolf Loos in 1910-12.*

STALLBURG

(IMPERIAL STABLE)

Built as a dwelling for the future Emperor Maximilian II in 1558, the imperial stable was, however, used as a stable as well as as a gallery for works of art. In 1955 the Renaissance colonnades which for 300 years had remained walled into the courtyard were brought to light. The ground floor still accommodates the stables of the *Spanische Reitschule* (Spanish Riding School). In addition, the *Neue Galerie* (New Art Gallery) of the *Kunsthistorisches Museum* has also been housed here, in a purpose-built area.

SPANISCHE REITSCHULE

(SPANISH RIDING SCHOOL)

In 1735 the young Fischer von Erlach completed the *Winterreitschule* (Winter Riding School), in which the famous exhibitions, particular to Vienna, of classical artistic horse-riding take place. The riders of the Spanish Riding School, in their traditional brown uniform, ride Lipizzaner horses, noble thoroughbreds, which were raised in "Lipizza" from 1580. Today this task has been taken over by the Piber Federal Stables, in Styria. The majestic hall of the winter Riding School, with its

Saeulengalerie (Gallery of the columns) and with the Hofloge (Imperial Loggia), in which one can admire an equestrian image of Emperor Charles VI (J.G. Hamilton - J.G. Auerbach), was the venue for solemn ceremonies and brilliant court feasts, also at the time of the Congress of Vienna.

JOSEFSPLATZ

(JOSEPH II SQUARE)

The hub of the square, which is closed off in an unusual way from the architectural point of view, is embodied by the equestrian monument of Josef II (F.A. Zauner, 1807). It is closed off on the right by the Redoutensäle (Lounge Rooms), rooms for concerts and ceremonies, and on the left by the Nationalbibliothek (National Library).

Commissioned by Emperor Charles VI as an imperial library (architects: Johann Bernhard and Joseph Emanuel Fischer von Erlach, 1723-35), and later enlarged with the fascinating library of Prince Eugène, it contains today more than 2.2 million works, both handwritten and printed. The dome of what may perhaps be considered as the most beautiful library in the world, contains a fresco in honour of Charles VI (the work of Daniel Grans, 1730). The marble statues of the commissioner of the construction and his predecessors, are older (1700, Peter and Paul Strudel).

Above: *Josefsplatz, the statue of Joseph II by F.A. Zauner.*
Below: *The interior of the Prunksaal in the National Library.*

AUGUSTINERKIRCHE

(Parish Church of Saint Augustine)
(1, Augustinerstrasse; Entrance: Josefsplatz)

This venerable church of the order of the hermits of Saint Augustine, consecrated in 1349, was elevated to Court Parish Church in 1634. After becoming City Parish Church in 1783, Ferdinand von Hohenberg began to renovate the Baroque interior in the Gothic style. He also moved the Loretto chapel, which originally stood at the centre of the church, to the side nave.

It is here that we find - in the *Herzgrueftel* (the so-called crypt of the hearts), 54 silver urns containing the hearts of many members of the House of Habsburg (from Ferdinand II, who died in 1637, to Francis Charles, father of Emperor Francis Joseph I, who died in 1878).

In the *Georgkapelle*, which dates back to the period of the construction, on the right next to the choir illustrious personages are buried (van Swieten, Maria Theresa's physician, and General Daun, who defeated Kolin).

The marble tomb of Archduchess Marie Christine (1742-98), daughter of Maria Theresa and consort of Duke Albert of Sachsen-Teschen (founder of the Albertina) is the work of A. Canova. "Uxori optimae, Albertus" (the best of wives, Albert), is the inscription above the door of a pyramid, in which we can observe allegorical figures of Virtue and Christian Love. The *Augustinerkirche* was the church where numerous royal weddings of the House of Habsburg were celebrated: for example the marriage of Joseph II and Isabella of Parma, or that of Francis Joseph and Elizabeth.

Above: *Danubius-Brunnen, in the background the massive Albertina building.*
Below: *Detail of the Danubius-Brunnen.*

ALBERTINA

(1, Augustinerstrasse 1)

The Baroque Taroucca building was rebuilt in 1801-04 for Duke Albert von Sachsen-Teschen, consort of Marie Christine, daughter of Maria Theresa.

J. Kornhäusel was responsible for the interior Neo-classical architecture on behalf of the couple's heir, Archduke Charles who defeated Napoleon at Aspern in 1809.

Duke Albert founded, together with Count Durazzo, the *Graphische Sammlung Albertina* (Albertina Graphic Collection) of worldwide fame, which numbers around 44,000 watercolours and drawings, and 1.5 million reproductions, ranging from the Gothic period to the present day.

The monument to Archduke Albert, the work of C. Zumbusch, is of 1899 and recalls the son of Archduke Charles and victor of the last great battle against the Italians in 1866 at Custoza.

Viktor Tilgner's statue of Mozart was placed in the Burggarten in 1953.

BURGGARTEN

(IMPERIAL GARDEN)
(between the New Imperial Palace and the Goetheg.)

This was located in 1818, together with the *Volksgarten* (Public Garden), in the area vacated by the blowing-up of the bastion, and initially was known as the *Kaisergarten* (garden of the emperor). Among the monuments worthy of mention are those dedicated to Mozart, to Francis Joseph I, to Francis I...

A greenhouse in Art Nouveau style.

SCHMETTERLINGHAUS

(BUTTERFLY HOUSE)
(1, Burggarten)

This exceptional glass house, in Art Nouveau style, contains all the enchantment of a tropical forest inhabited by thousands of butterflies of myriad different species. The visitor here is literally transported into a fantastic world made of animals, plants, gigantic trees, and even waterfalls and pools.

KAPUZINERKIRCHE AND THE KAISERGRUFT

(CHURCH OF THE CAPUCHINS AND IMPERIAL CRYPT)
(I, Neuer Markt)

Under the modest *Kapuzinerkirche* (Church of the Capuchins) lies, tended by the Capuchin order, the tomb of many members of the Habsburg dynasty officially buried here, including 10 emperors and 15 empresses. Emperor Matthias and his consort Anna, the Founders (1618) were not able to be present at the construction of the crypt (1632). Throughout the 20th century extension works have been underway.

It consists of various rooms: the *Gründergruft* (crypt of the foundation), the *Leopoldinische Gruft* (Leopoldine crypt), the *Karolinische Gruft* (Carolingian crypt - Leopold I and Joseph I in the sarcophagi created to a design by L. v. Hildebrandt; Charles VI in a sarcophagus by Balthasar Moll), the *Maria-Theresien-Gruft* (Maria Theresa crypt - double sarcophagus for Maria Theresa and Francis Stephen of Lorraine, by B. Moll 1753, constructed during the reign of the imperial couple; tomb of Joseph II), the *Franzengruft* (crypt of Francis I), the *Ferdinandgruft* (crypt of Emperor Ferdinand), the *Toskanagruft*, the *Franz-Josef-Gruft* (Francis Joseph, Empress Elizabeth, Crown Prince Rudolf), the *Neue Gruft* (new crypt) and the Chapel where the last empress lies, Zita, who died in 1989.

PALAIS TRAUTSON

(TRAUTSON PALACE)
(7, Museumstrasse 7)

J.B. Fischer von Erlach built this palace, between 1709 and 1712, for Prince Donat Trautson, previously the court steward of Emperor Joseph I. Little remains of the interior. In 1961 the palace became the seat of the Ministry of Justice.

Top: *the Kapuzinerkirche or Capuchin Church).* **Center:** *the Kaisergruft or Imperial Crypt with (from left to right) the tombs of Empress Elisabeth, Emperor Franz Joseph, and Crown Prince Rudolph.* **Left:** *Trautson Palace.*

MINORITENKIRCHE

(CHURCH OF THE FRIARS MINOR)
Maria Schnee
(1, Minoritenplatz)

From 1330 to 1380 the Friars Minor of Saint Francis of Assisi, who arrived in Vienna in 1230, constructed on the walls of their old church, the sacred building which still today constitutes the nucleus of the Church of the Friars Minor. In 1784 it was given to the Italian anti-Joseph Congregation of the Madonna of the Snow. From 1957 onwards, the Friars Minor were responsible for caring for the church, which from 1784 to 1789 was renovated in the Gothic style.

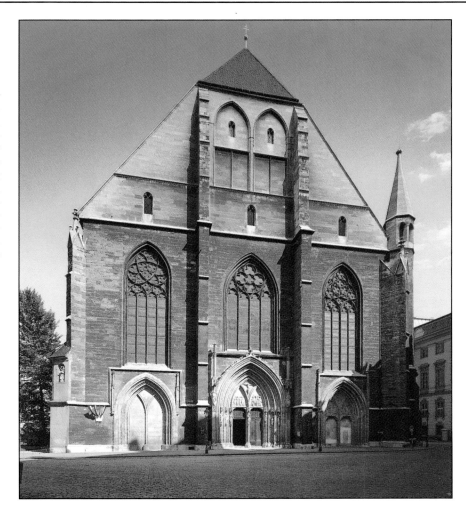

VOLKSTHEATER

(PEOPLE'S THEATRE)
(7, Neustiftgasse 1)

The People's Theatre (built in 1887-89 by F. Fellner and H. Helmer), in many ways represented a new type of theatre. With its works which range from traditional Viennese popular Neo-classicism to avant-garde performances, an effort has always been made to reach every social class. The monument to Ferdinand Raimund (F. Vogl, 1898), situated in the nearby *Weghuberpark*, reminds us of the popular classical writer Raimund (1790-1836) who, in the period of pre-revolutionary Vienna, devised a different and better world, which he described in his imaginative works.

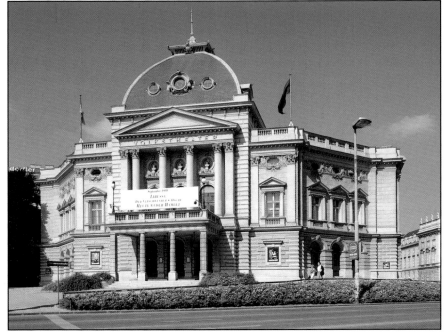

Top: *the Minoritenkirche or Church of the Friars Minor.*
Bottom: *the Volkstheater.*

KARLSKIRCHE

(CHURCH OF SAINT CHARLES)
(4, Karlsplatz)

In 1713, Emperor Charles VI, when Vienna was devastated by the plague, made a vow to his homonymous patron saint, Saint Carlo Borromeo, to construct a church if the epidemic should finish. The real imperial church of Saint Charles was, however, built by Johann Bernard Fischer von Erlach and represents his last and most important work. The final phase of its construction, though, was carried out by his son Joseph Emanuel, who completed it in 1739.

The way in which it is designed shows the clear influence of Greek and Roman architecture, as well as that of France and Italy. In front of the central body, surmounted by a majestic dome, 72 m high, we find a colonnade which recalls the style of ancient temples. Two triumphal columns flank the pediment, similar to the Trajan Columns in Rome, and along their shaft run spiralling reliefs narrating the life of Saint Carlo Borromeo (J. Christoph Mader).

The central body is delimited on either side by two bell-towers. The interiors were created by the greatest artists of the age: it is enough to mention the fresco in the dome depicting the "Glories of S. Borromeo" by Rottmayr, or the Altar-piece by D. Grans in the *Taufkapelle* (baptistry) on the left of the entrance, or the High Altar by J.B. Fischer von Erlach. Since 1738 the church has been under the care of the Order of the *Kreuzherren* (Knights of the Holy Cross).

SECESSION

(1, Friedrichstrasse 12)

On 22nd May 1897 a group of nineteen Viennese artists founded the "*Vereinigung bildender Künstler Österreichs Secession*" (Secession Movement of Austrian Figurative Artists). Among these we find Josef Hoffmann, Gustav Klimt, Joseph Maria Olbrich and Otto Wagner. Olbrich, pupil of Hasenauer and of Otto Wagner, erected in 1897-98 the construction in which the group's work was exhibited, a building also known as "*Secession*" and on whose door is the inscription "To time its art, to art its freedom".

Klimt designed the metal doors which, unfortunately, have not survived. This "home of art" with its cubic forms is surmounted by a dome made of laurel branches in gilded metal, which was irreverently nicknamed "*Krauthappel*" - bite of cabbage. A room on the ground floor has been set aside for the "Beethoven Frieze", a work by Gustav Klimt executed in 1902, to mark the 75th anniversary of the great master's death.

Above: *Relief on the facade of the Secession.*
Below: *Secession Building. This original building is shaped like a flattened cube with four towers and a roof surmounted by a gold dome.*

THEATER AN DER WIEN

(THEATRE ON THE RIVER WIEN)
(6, Linke Wienzeile 6)

Emanuel Schikaneder, the librettist of Mozart's "Magic Flute", had a theatre built in Vienna in 1798-1801 which subsequently was to number among the best-loved buildings in the city. Beethoven wrote his only opera "Fidelio" for the *Theater an der Wien* and his Concerto for Violin was also performed here for the first time, as were works by Kleist, Grillparzer, Nestroy etc. The Magic Flute had already been performed in the old theatre in 1791. In the so-called golden age of operetta (Strauss, Milloecker, Zeller) and in the silver age (Lehàr, Eysler, Kàlmàn), what was defined as the "house of light Music" was often used. Today the *Theater an der Wien* is considered to be one of the most important theatres of music in Europe.

WIENZEILE-HÄUSER

(HOUSES BY OTTO WAGNER)
(6, Linke Wienzeile 40 and 38)

In 1898 Otto Wagner commissioned the construction, partly at his own expense, of two buildings which, with their multi-coloured facades, were the answer to his architectural ideas; the chosen site was the *Wienzeile*, which at the time had been designed as a luxurious street leading from the Imperial Palace to Schönbrunn. Kolo Moser was responsible for the decoration of the building at no. 38, whilst the building at no. 40, the *Majolika Haus* (Majolica House, whose name derives from the Majorcan ceramics used in its realization), charms and seduces with its red floral decorations.

Above: *The entrance to the Theater an der Wien.*
Below: *Detail of the facade of the Majolika Haus.*

MUSIKVEREIN

(MUSICAL ASSOCIATION)
(1, Dumbastrasse 3)

The Great Hall, or Golden Hall of the "Society of the Friends of Music" building, also known as *Musikverein* (built by Th. Hansen in 1867-69), is without doubt the hub of Viennese musical life. It is, so to speak, the home of the Viennese Philharmonic, whose New Year Concert is broadcast from here on television to many countries worldwide. Both the musicians and the audience praise the incomparable acoustics of this hall. The *"Gesellschaft der Musikfreunde des Oesterreichisches Kaiserstaates"* (Association of the Friends of Music of the Imperial Austrian State), owns a large History of Music collection, including priceless original autographs, scores, instruments and pieces which are a significant reminder of the great masters of music.

Above: *The Gold Hall of the Musikverein.*
Below: *The facade of the Musikverein.*

SCHÖNBRUNN

This is without doubt one of the most visited places in Vienna. Even though the real political centre of the Kingdom of the Habsburgs has always been the Imperial Palace in Vienna, the Schönbrunn residence has become the symbol of the "good old days", thanks to its combination of domestic and political features.

In 1683 the Turks so utterly destroyed both the *Katterburg* (where Maximilian II at one time kept exotic animals) and the more recent *Lustschloss* of Eleonora Gonzaga, widow of Emperor Ferdinand II, that it was not worth while rebuilding them. Then Emperor Leopold I commissioned J. Bernhard Fischer von Erlach to design a new imperial castle for hunting purposes.

After a design had been drawn up which surpassed even Versailles in majesty and sumptuousness, in 1696 the construction of a symmetrical central body with two side wings got underway. In the part which looks out towards the city a courtyard of honour was created, surrounded by stables, whilst opposite the present-day Gloriette hill a magnificent park was designed by Jean Trehet.

In 1700, the castle, although not yet completed, was inhabited. Building works progressed under Emperor Joseph I, but under Charles VI, who thought more about enlarging the *Klosterneuburg* than the imperial residence, these were considerably neglected. Subsequently, it was Maria Theresa (1740-80), who had a great love for Schönbrunn, who commissioned Nikolaus Pacassi and the builder Valmagini to transform the castle into an imperial summer residence (1743-49). Pacassi completely renovated the most representative centre of the building, adding the Large and Small Gallery; near the latter were situated the Round Cabinet and the Oval Cabinet. The entrance in the courtyard created by Fischer, was replaced by Pacassi with an elegant staircase supported by pillars with a balustrade which acts as an entrance and a passage for the ground floor. The architect had a small roof and a slope built on the castle and given that it was necessary to create more space for the numerous visits of the court, he added an intermediate storey.

In 1747 the *Schlosstheater* (Castle Theatre) was added to the western courtyard of honour. Members of the Imperial House often took an active part in the operatic and theatrical performances staged there. In 1751 Jean Jadot began to build the Menagerie, the zoological garden. The vaults added by Pacassi to both galleries were frescoed by Gregorio Guglielmi, whilst Albert G. Bolla created the stuccos (1761). These Entertaining Rooms constitute the essence of Austrian Roco-

co, an epoch which took its name from 'rocaille', a typical frieze in the form of a shell. This style is evident in the Small and Large Gallery, in the Chinese Rooms (Oval and Round Cabinet, the Million Room and the Antique Lacquer Room), in the private rooms (Porcelain Room, Miniatures Room, "Landscape Room") and in the *Schlosstheater*, renovated with great artistic taste by J. Ferdinand von Hohenberg in 1766-67.

In addition to the other areas of green, such as the *Kronprinzgarten* (garden of the crown prince) and the *Kammergarten* (garden of the chamber), which are on the right and left of the castle, or the *Holländischer Garten* (Dutch garden) and the *Orangerie* (the orangery) set up

Above: *the Gloriette with the Neptune Fountain.*
Below: *the Gloriette.*
Right-hand page: *Schönbrunn - Fountain of the Naiads.*

in 1755, the superb present-day park represents the realization of the Neo-classical ideals of the Hohenbergs (from 1765) and the plastic inspiration of the group of sculptors who collaborated with Wilhelm Beyer from 1772 onwards.

The four parallel paths through the park are cut across by two diagonals: the left-hand one leads to the *Obeliskenkaskade* (obelisk cascade), the right-hand one to the *Tiergarten* (zoological garden). In 1775 the Gloriette colonnade was built, the great work of Hohenberg, which surrounds the entire park. There follow the *Obeliskenkaskade*, (or *Sibyllengrotte* (grotto of the Sybil, 1777) and the *Römische Ruine* (Roman ruin, 1778). The *Taubenhaus* (dovecote) and the *Kleine Gloriette* (little Gloriette) also belong to this period. The statues of the *Neptunbrunnen* (fountain of Neptune) at the foot of the *Gloriette-Hügel* (Gloriette hill) are the work of Franz A. Zauner, the *Najadengruppe* (group of naiads) in the fishponds along the diagonal paths are also the work of Beyer.

Left-hand page: *The Million Room.* On this page, right: "*Vieux-Lacque*" Room, decorated with elegant oriental panels.
Below: *The old winter stables house the historical Collection of Imperial Carriages.*

Essentially, the left-hand area of the park is designed as an ornamental garden, while the right-hand area has assumed scientific importance, which is why it contains the zoological garden, the botanical garden and the *Palmenhaus* (palm house) built in 1882. In 1805 and again in 1809, the triumphant Napoleon stayed temporarily at Schönbrunn, and it is here that his son, Napoleon François Joseph, Duke of Reichstadt, lived with Marie Louise, daughter of Emperor Francis, until his premature death from tuberculosis in 1832. In 1940 his body was removed from the *Kapuzinergruft*, the Capuchin crypt, and taken to the cathedral of Les Invalides in Paris.

During the Congress of Vienna (1814-15), as also on the occasion of the *Wiener Weltausstellung* of 1873 (Viennese World Fair), Schönbrunn was often the venue for splendid festivals. Francis Joseph I was born here in 1830 and chose this residence ever more frequently as his place of work. He died here in 1916, during the First World War. It was here that his successor Charles I renounced the throne in 1918, thus putting an end to the monarchy in Austria. In 1955 the *Staatsvertrag* (State Treaty), giving back Austria its freedom, was sanctioned at Schönbrunn. The summit between Kennedy and Kruschev in 1961, continued the castle's tradition for being the venue of some of the most important international meetings.

Left-hand page: *The Large Gallery, still used today for State receptions.*
Below: *Palmenhaus (Palm House).*

Roman ruins: Triumphal Arch.

SYNAGOGE

(THE SYNAGOGUE)
(1, Seitenstettengasse)

A barely visible inscription above the door indicates that we have before us one of the most important Jewish temples in Vienna. According to Joseph II's building regulations, no non-Christian church could show its facade towards the street, which is why Joseph Kornhäusel modified the synagogue, building inside it the Complex of the *Kultusgemeinde* (Community of worship), erected in 1826.

Of the 20 synagogues in Vienna, this was the only one not to be destroyed by the Nazis during *Reichskristallnacht* (Crystal Night) between the 9th and 10th November 1938.

RUPRECHTSKIRCHE

(THE CHURCH OF RUPERT)
(1, Ruprechtsplatz)

It is considered to be the oldest church in Vienna. It was in fact built in 740, but a large part of the present-day church dates back to the 11th century, while the median window of the choir is of the 13th century.

GRIECHENBEISL

(1, Griechengasse 9)

It is said that the renowned ballad singer Augustine, known as *Lieber Augustin* wrote his most famous song "O *du lieber Augustin, alles ist hin...*" (O dear Augustine, all is lost...) in this inn no less, at the time of the 1679 plague. The colony of Greek merchants, who in the 18th century lived in the surrounding area, gave this name to the inn. The many illustrious guests bear witness to its gastronomic reputation.

Above: *Ruprechtskirche.*
Left: *Detail of the Greek Tavern (Griechenbeisl)*

BELVEDERE

(Upper: 3, Prinz-Eugen-Str. 27, Lower: 3, Rennweg 6)

Prince Eugène of Savoy (1663-1736), known as "The Sword of the Habsburgs" because of his successes against the Turks, being a highly knowledgeable patron of the arts, commissioned Johann Lucas von Hildebrandt to build the summer residence of the Belvedere, consisting of two buildings.
He financed the project with the proceeds obtained from his glorious military campaigns and with the revenues of his lieutenancy in the Netherlands. The splendid garden is the work of the Bavarian, Dominique Girard. The complex was more or less completed in 1725.
The Upper Belvedere was used for hosting entertainments, while the Lower one was used as the prince's summer residence. Immediately after his death, it passed into the possession of the House of the Habsburgs. Towards 1775, Joseph II housed the *Gemäldesammlung* (court art collection) here, augmented in 1806 with a collection originating from the castle of Ambras, in the Tirol, which under Napoleon had become Bavarian. In 1890 these collections were taken to the recently-built *Kunsthistorisches Museum* on the Ring.

The successor to the throne, Franz Ferdinand, temporarily resided in the Upper Belvedere from 1894, before his assassination in Sarajevo. Anton Bruckner lived for a short period, until his death in 1896, in the *Kustodentrakt* (custodians' wing), in the adjacent building.
On 15th May 1955 in the Marble Room of the Upper Belvedere the Austrian State Treaty was signed by the Foreign Ministers Dulles (USA), Macmillan (GB), Molotov (Russia), Pinay (F), and Figl (Austria), a treaty which placed an end to the occupation of the country by the victorious powers of the Second World War.
Today the Belvedere is part of the Austrian Gallery. The Lower Belvedere houses the *Österreichische Barockmuseum* (Austrian Baroque Mu-

Right-hand page, above: *Baroque portal of the Upper Belvedere.*
Below: *The Upper Belvedere Palace.*

Above: *Upper Belvedere.*
Below: *Upper Belvedere: the Earthly Room, in which telamones support the vaults.*
Right-hand page: *The monumental staircase of the Marble Room.*

seum) which provides an overall view of the sculpture and painting of the 17th-18th century; in the Orangery we find the *Museum österrechischer mittelalterlicher Kunst* (Austrian museum of mediaeval art), with works ranging from the 12th to the 16th century.

The Upper Belvedere houses the *Galerie des 19. und 20. Jahrhunderts* (Gallery of the 19th and 20th century), with sections dedicated to Classicism, Biedermeier, the Ringstrasse Style, the Jugendstil and, in addition, it houses the greatest collection of the works of Gustav Klimt, Egon Schiele and Oscar Kokoschka, artists whose works influenced and inspired modern art beyond the Austrian borders.

The Upper Belvedere houses a collection of 19th and 20th century paintings.
Below: Egon Schiele - "Mother with children".
Right-hand page: Gustav Klimt - The Embrace.

The Belvedere houses the largest collection of Klimt's works.
Above: "Water snakes" (1904-1907).
Centre: Adele Bloch-Bauer (II) (1912).
Opposite, above: Adele Bloch-Bauer (1907).
Below: "Woman with hat and feather boa" (1909).

Lower Belvedere: Hall of the Grotesques – Jonas Drentwett.
Lower Belvedere: Hall of Mirrors.

Top: *an aerial view of the Lower Belvedere and the Upper Belvedere.*   **Bottom:** *the facade of the Lower Belvedere.*

HUNDERTWASSERHAUS

(HUNDERTWASSER HOUSE)
(3, Löwengasse)

Friedensreich Hundertwasser, well-known painter and Academy professor, motivated by a total rejection of the geometric flatness and excessive linearity in architecture, with this house in the Municipality of Vienna, completed in 1985, realized his stylistic and ecological ambitions.

Left: *detail of the facade of the Kunst Haus Wien where a permanent exhibition by the painting master Hundertwasser can be seen.*
Below: *details of the Hundertwasserhaus.*
Right-hand page: *Hundertwasserhaus, view of Kegelgasse.*

KARL-MARX-HOF

(19, Heiligenstädterstrasse)

The building, erected by Karl Ehn between 1927 and 1930, with its long facade around 1,200 m long, and with its 1600 flats, is the most representative example of popular building in "red" Vienna between the two world wars.

FAVORITNER WASSERTURM

(FAVORITNER WATER TOWER)
(10, Wienerberg)

The rapid growth of the city of Vienna caused notable problems for the water supply. The numerous domestic wells were often the breeding-ground for cholera epidemics. With the implementation of the First (1873) and the Second (1910) high spring aqueduct, originating from the area of the Rax or of the Schneeberg, namely from the area of the *Hochschwab* and the *Wildalpen*, this problem was solved once and for all. The *Favoritner Wasserturm*, which from 1899 to 1910 functioned as a hydro-centre, has now become a panoramic tower and provides a fine example of how even industrial architecture may have its own brand of charm.

ARSENAL

(THE ARSENAL)
(3, Arsenalstrasse)

In 1848 the revolutionaries had been able to take up arms in the court arsenal with comparative ease. To avoid the repetition of a similar occurrence in future, in 1849-55 an arsenal in the shape of a fortress was erected.

The *Heeresgeschichtlichen Museum* (Military History Museum) which was housed here with its *Ruhmeshalle* (Hall of Glories) and the *Feldherrnhalle* (Hall of Generals), is to a large extent the work of Th. Hansen. In the *Sarajevo-Raum* (Sarajevo Room) the blood-stained uniform and the vehicle in which Crown Prince Franz Ferdinand was assassinated in 1914 in Sarajevo, are on display.

Right: *The Hall of the Generals.*
Below: *The facade of the Arsenal.*

PRATER

(In the 2nd district)

After Emperor Joseph II had official-ly opened the royal hunting reserve of the *Praterauen* (Prater park) to the public in 1766, this area soon be-came a public meeting and walking place for the Viennese. Cafès, kiosks and restaurants were opened and the "W*urstelprater*" of-fered entertainments of all sorts for young and old alike.

In 1897 the *Riesenrad* (panoramic wheel) was constructed. After hav-ing been destroyed during the Sec-ond World War (1945), the Wurstel-prater was entirely rebuilt in the modern style. Between the Riesen-rad and the *Praterstadion* (Prater sta-dium) runs a *Lilliputbahn* (miniature railway); swings, roundabouts, shooting arcades, the ghost train and house of mirrors provide end-less fun - and not just for the chil-dren!

WIENER RIESENRAD

The Wiener Riesenrad was built in 1896-97 by the English engineer Walter B. Basset. Towards the end of the war, in 1945, this symbol of Vienna was destroyed, including its cages and electrical system. Only two years later, however, the Riesenrad began to revolve once again round its axis, half a metre thick and ten metres long, though the number of cages was halved. From these slowly-revolving cages, you can enjoy a marvellous panoramic view of the city.

Some technical facts:

The diameter of the wheel is 61 m; the highest point is at 64.75 m; the entire construction, with its 120 spokes, weighs 430.05 tons.

Views from the Prater.

FRANZ-VON-ASSISI-KIRCHE

(COMMEMORATIVE CHURCH OF THE JUBILEE OF FRANCIS JOSEPH)
(2, Mexicoplatz 12)

The church was built between 1898 and 1913 on the occasion of the 50th Jubilee of the reign of Emperor Francis Joseph. The brick construction also houses a commemorative chapel, on the model of the *Aachener Pfalzkapelle* (Palatine chapel of Aachen) dedicated to the Empress Elizabeth.

ISLAMISCHES ZENTRUM

(THE ISLAMIC CENTRE)
(21, am Hubertusdamm 17-19)

The Islamic centre includes a Large and a Small Mosque, a Koran School and a library.

DONAUINSEL

(DANUBE ISLAND)

Despite the plan for regulating the Danube dating back to the 19th century, the river was often full. For this reason, in 1972, a reduction millrace was dug, thus creating an island about 20 km long, which immediately became a public meeting and walking place. It has, among other things, the advantage of being easily reached by underground train.

UNO-CITY

(UNITED NATIONS CITY)
(22nd district)

In 1979, the United Nations set up its third seat in Vienna, after New York and Geneva. In the Vienna International Center, (built in 1973-79 by the architect Joh. Staber), employees of the United Nations from more than 100 countries now work.

UNO-City - (Vienna International Centre) Built in the seventies as the headquarters for the international organizations present in Vienna.

DONAU-CITY

Vienna Donau-City, directly overlooking the Danube, is one of the most modern complexes in the city and one of Austria's most brilliant development projects.

The development is of particular importance due to its proximity to the Vienna International Center (UNO-City) and to the Austria Center Vienna. Projects of the caliber of the Andromeda Tower, the Ares Tower, the Tech Gate Vienna, and the Mischek Tower (to name only a few) cover an area of 17.5 hectares. Vienna Donau-City has become an authentic point of reference for culture and free time alike, with its offices, housing, and shops—but also educational and research institutions.

MILLENIUM-TOWER

(20, Handelskai 94-96)
La Millennium-Tower, with its 50 floors to a height of 202 meters, is the tallest building in all of Austria and indeed one of Europe's tallest buildings designed for office use. The surrounding Millennium-City is the milieu for more than 50 public establishments (shops, restaurants, and bars), besides housing and offices.

DONAUTURM

(DANUBE TOWER - DANUBE PARK)

The tower, 252 m high, was constructed in 1964 for the *Wiener Internationaler Gartenausstellung* (International Viennese Gardens Exhibition) together with the *Donaupark* (Danube park) which extends for more than 1 km sq. (architect H. Lintl; statics: R. Krapfenbauer).
Its Belvedere terrace is situated at an altitude of 150 m and at 169 m is a slowly-revolving restaurant which, at affordable prices, makes the Donauturm a gastronomic attraction as well. In addition, the tower contains a *Wiener Kaffeehaus*, Viennese Coffee-house. The complex is easily reached by lift in a matter of a few seconds.

GRINZING

(19th district)

The ancient village of *Grinzing* was incorporated into the municipality of Vienna in 1892 and of all the localities in the *Heurig*, such as *Sievering*, *Nussdorf*, *Salmannsdorf* and *Neustift am Walde* for example, it is the one which has best preserved its typical character as a "vine-dressers' village".

Much of the atmospheric and picturesque centre of the village dates back to the 16th and 17th century. According to an ancient privilege, the grape gatherers can serve their own wine in the bars, especially in the case of the *Heuriger*, vin nouveau, which is not more than one year old. The expression 'A*usg'steckt ist*' means that if there is a branch of Scotch pine (*buschen*) hanging on the door of a harvester's house, it indicates that this is a typical bar of the Viennese *Heuriger*, and offers home-made wines exclusively.

Below: *the church in Grinzing.*

KAHLENBERG AND LEOPOLDSBERG

(19th district)

Kahlenberg and *Leopoldsberg* are the final slopes of the *Wiener Wald* and of the Austrian Alps therefore.

In Leopoldsberg, in the building under construction of the *Leopoldskirche* (church of Leopold), on the morning of 12th September 1683, before the battle against the Turks who once again had occupied Vienna, the Papal legate, Marco d'Aviano, said mass for Leopold I's army (the Polish King Jan Sobieski served at the mass). The victory of the troops of the Holy Roman Empire averted the danger of an Is-

lamization of Europe.

The *Sobieski-Kapelle* (Sobieski Chapel) in the *St. Josef Kirche* (Church of St. Joseph) in *Kahlenberg* recalls this event. Both areas can easily be reached by a bus service and, as well as the atmospheric views, they also offer excellent local food.

Above: *the St. Josef Kirche in Kahlenberg.*
Below: *The Leopoldskirche in Leopoldsberg.*

THE SEEGROTTE (LAKE GROTTO) AT HINTERBRÜHL

Lower Austria, not far from Mödling (south of Vienna).
In 1912, following an explosion, this chalk mine was inundated by more than 20 million liters of water, forming the largest subterranean lake in Europe.. After the catastrophe, the mine was closed, but in the 1930's a group of speleologists rediscovered it and led efforts to make it accessible to the public. The "Lake Grotto" was literally requisitioned during World War II, and it was here that the first fighter plane in all of world aviation was built. After the war, it was again opened to the public and today is an important tourist attraction.

Top right: *a boat excursion on the subterranean lake.*
Bottom left: *aircraft production in the WW II period.*

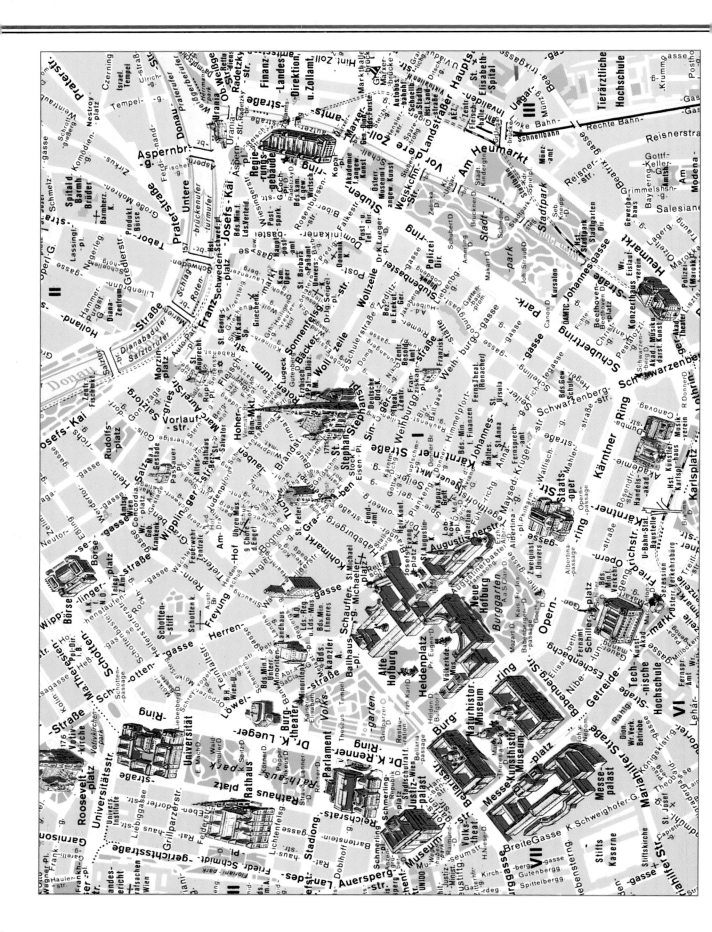